AF808908

Immigration and Economic Recovery after COVID-19

Paperback ISBN: 978-1-7348561-4-9

eISBN: 978-1-7348561-5-6

The Center for Growth and Opportunity at Utah State University
3525 Old Main Hill
Logan, UT 84322
www. thecgo.org

Cover design and typesetting by Brooke Jacques

Immigration and Economic Recovery after COVID-19

Edited by Josh T. Smith

The Center for
Growth and **Opportunity**
at Utah State University

CONTENTS

PREFACE

How Immigration Brings Prosperity

Josh T. Smith

Peter Tsai grew up in Taiwan. He moved to the United States in 1981 to start an engineering doctorate at Kansas State University. In 1995, he patented the technology for N95 masks. In August of 2019, the University of Tennessee estimated that more than one billion people had used the N95 masks to protect themselves from diseases such as SARS and swine flu.[1] Once COVID-19 is included, that number is certain to be much higher.

Dr. Tsai's work is a standout example of immigrant-made contributions to America's success. Some of America's most valuable companies grew out of ideas from immigrants. Google, Yahoo, Uber, and Tesla are prime examples. Historical examples include Andrew Carnegie's steel and railway empire, and AT&T, started as Bell Telephone Company, founded by Alexander Graham Bell, the American-Scottish inventor of the telephone.

These aren't just anecdotes. Research on immigration clearly finds that immigrants play a vital role in driving entrepreneurship and innovation.[2] This role has proven to be even more important during a pandemic. Immigrants make up an outsized share of frontline, essential workers in industries critical to responding to COVID-19, like healthcare.

Despite immigrants' critical role, the pandemic triggered limits on immigration to the United States. At the beginning of the pandemic, certain travel restrictions made sense, as scientists hurried to understand the new contagion and as leaders attempted to slow the spread of the disease. But eventually, these restrictions will be rolled back. That return to openness and cooperation must include a renewed appreciation for immigrants and their contributions to our nation.

Consider the story of the Pfizer-BioNTech vaccine's development. It was created by Turkish immigrants working for a US company while living in Germany. The unprecedented pace of the vaccine's development was possible only because of 30 years of prior research by biochemist Katalin Karikó, a Hungarian immigrant working at the University of Pennsylvania.[3] As Charles Kenny, the author of *The Plague Cycle*, points out, "you can't make it more obvious how important globalization is to the speed of our response."[4]

Effective disease responses require a cooperative, global effort. The world is connected in ways that make collaboration indispensable in times of crisis as well as integral to the modern world's prosperity. Short-term separation is a prudent response to disease as we learn about the risks and potential treatments. But prolonged separation will never lead to a long-term success story. For example, researchers at the Center for Global Development analyzed four past pandemics and showed that even a 50 percent reduction in international mobility will only delay the arrival of the disease by one or two weeks.[5]

Defenders of openness during these critical times have a heavy task ahead. Withdrawal and isolation are innate responses to disease, even if that approach is poorly suited to the modern world. As part of the effort to turn the tide, we have prepared this collection of essays reflecting the research and policy advice of some of the top immigration researchers in the world. Each chapter points to different ways that immigrants contribute to prosperity. All of the essays confirm the importance of immigration in creating a strong recovery from COVID-19 by revealing how immigration brings prosperity.

William Kerr's essay discusses the importance of foreign students, like Peter Tsai, in maintaining economic growth. That idea is echoed by Pia Orrenius and Madeline Zavodny's essay, pointing out how increased immigration boosts America's long-term prosperity and global success. Likewise, Sari Pekkala Kerr's chapter delves into the role immigrant entrepreneurs play in promoting prosperity.

The Hoover Institution's economist Tim Kane brings an international perspective with his simple argument that people are power—not just for the innovative ideas that immigrant students and entrepreneurs bring to the United States, but also as a simple measure of a country's success.

At a more local level, Giovanni Peri's essay discusses the indispensable role of immigrant workers in industries like agriculture and healthcare that keep the world fed and healthy. And Margaret Peters shows that welcoming refugees can revive local communities by bringing in workers for existing businesses as well as people who start new enterprises.

Dr. Peters's essay shares a common thread with economist Kimberly Clausing's chapter on the need for openness. The restrictions on movement that made sense at the onset of the COVID-19 pandemic must be undone in order to restore and enhance the free flow of goods and people that enrich the modern world. In fact, lockdowns and travel restrictions represent microcosms of the losses that the entire world faces because of the restrictions on the movement of people. Fundamentally, more openness will create more prosperity.

Immigration economist Catalina Amuedo-Dorantes also writes on the need for openness. Specifically, Dr. Amuedo-Dorantes explains the benefits of including immigrants in our responses to diseases. Because immigrants work and live next to native-born citizens, protecting immigrants protects the health of entire communities.

Three of the essays give broad advice on reforming immigration policy both during a pandemic and going forward. The Institute for Immigration Research's Michele Waslin and James Witte give a broad call to remember that immigration is a positive-sum game. Immigration policy goes off course whenever it forgets that immigration grows wealth for everyone in the long run. Historian Alan Kraut's essay calls for rethinking the immigration system to ensure that those long-term gains are maximized and that businesses find the workers they need.

Neeraj Kaushal, the author of *Blaming Immigrants*, summarizes several lessons for future immigration policy from COVID-19's effects on supply chains. As she points out, even as borders were closing, Western countries were flying in immigrant workers to ensure that critical industries could continue operating.

Stepping outside of the world of policy questions, Chapman University philosophy professor Bas van der Vossen discusses the ethics of immigration and economic recovery. He points to the humanitarian argument for immigration but reminds us that "the case for relaxing immigration restrictions is also a self-interested one. It's by far the best thing we can do for the American economy." Dr. van der Vossen's chapter distills the major arguments from his book, *In Defense of Openness*, co-authored with Jason Brennan.

Jack Goldstone's chapter concludes with stories of immigration's role in producing the leaders of today in both the political world and the economic sphere. It's often forgotten that prominent leaders of both political parties today are the children of immigrants.

At the heart of each chapter are two simple interlocking ideas about the economy and the pandemic. First, we are in this together. Second, we are better together. Stories like Dr. Tsai's development of the N95 mask, as well as the international efforts behind the development of COVID-19 vaccines, illustrate these facts about the world. Policymakers will set the stage for a vibrant future of economic growth, opportunity, and prosperity when they work from these ideas.

I hope that you enjoy the research and policy suggestions from this edited volume. We are writing and supporting more research like this at the Center for Growth and Opportunity at Utah State University. You can see our most recent research and reach out to us through our website, *thecgo.org*.

Josh T. Smith is a Research Manager for the Center for Growth and Opportunity at Utah State University.

Endnotes

1 "UT Researcher's Nonwoven Fabrics Protect the Health of More Than a Billion People," August 27, 2019, UT Research Foundation, https://utrf.tennessee.edu/ut-researchers-nonwoven-fabrics-protect-the-health-of-more-than-a-billion-people/.

2 Jennifer Hunt and Marjolaine Gauthier-Loiselle, "How Much Does Immigration Boost Innovation?," *American Economic Journal: Macroeconomics* 2, no. 2 (2010): 31–56.

3 Damian Garde, "The story of mRNA: How a once-dismissed idea became a leading technology in the Covid vaccine race," November 10, 2010, *STAT*, https://www.statnews.com/2020/11/10/the-story-of-mrna-how-a-once-dismissed-idea-became-a-leading-technology-in-the-covid-vaccine-race/.

4 Charles Kenny, "COVID-19 and Cooperation: Why Openness Matters," interview by Josh T. Smith, The Center for Growth and Opportunity at Utah State University, March 1, 2021, https://www.thecgo.org/news/covid-19-and-cooperation-why-openness-matters/.

5 Michael Clemens and Thomas Ginn, "Global Mobility and the Threat of Pandemics: Evidence from Three Centuries," Center for Global Development, December 10, 2020, https://www.cgdev.org/publication/global-mobility-and-threat-pandemics-evidence-three-centuries.

CHAPTER 1

Students, Skilled Immigration, and Our Path to Recovery

William R. Kerr

The COVID-19 pandemic has made the economy suffer through a medically induced coma, with local businesses mostly shut down and international borders closed, in order to solve a public health emergency. We all want nonessential businesses to get back on their feet as soon as virus containment allows, but each passing month makes it harder for companies to survive and restore jobs and economic opportunity. Millions of people are waiting to be called back, and that call cannot come soon enough, despite the massive stimulus injected by the government.

The prospect of reopening borders and resuming global integration is even more in question, and rightly so. Global exchange could hasten additional virus outbreaks and surges. Tourism and foreign business travel will be important economic stimulants to our recovery—particularly for the hard-hit sectors of airlines, accommodation, leisure parks, and so on—but only if safety can be secured in these traditionally crowd-heavy industries. Others argue that our supply chains need to become more localized, especially for key items like personal protective equipment. Upcoming contracts issued by federal and state governments may contain domestic sourcing clauses, indicating a willingness to pay more for a lesser risk of globalized disruptions.

However we recalibrate global integration, we must protect some of the key advantages America and its economy gain through immigration. As of early June 2020, some policymakers were debating how they might halt vast parts of skilled migration into the country, with plans ranging from a moratorium on new foreign student visas to a suspension of temporary skilled immigration visa programs like the H-1B program. While these proposals are often presented as a thoughtful reaction to the crisis, most of the proponents of these policies expressed similar sentiments well before we ever heard the term "coronavirus." Indeed, these restrictions would be a mistake. A better course would be to use this crisis to make our skilled immigration system better and stronger, as it is long overdue for an overhaul.

US innovation and entrepreneurship rely heavily on foreign talent, with immigrants accounting for more than a quarter of our patents and new business start-ups. The end of May saw a vivid example as SpaceX became the first private company to launch astronauts into space; its founder, Elon Musk, is a South African who came to the United States for school by way of Canada. This type of vital global input is also part of the race against COVID-19. Moderna, one of the companies leading the race for a vaccine, has both an immigrant co-founder and an immigrant CEO. Many scientists working in the US pharmaceutical industry come from abroad, and the global scientific community is taking huge steps to cooperate in the vaccine race.

America has historically sat at the center of global talent exchanges, and it would be devastating to lose this special position. Figure 1, created using digital records that accompany patents, shows the net migration of inventors during the 2000–2010 decade. In those years, the United States received an astounding 57 percent of inventors moving globally. My book, *The Gift of Global Talent*, catalogs the other disproportionately large contributions immigrants make to our economy, ranging from winning Nobel Prizes (e.g., four of the eight Americans awarded the Nobel Prize in 2019 were immigrants; a fifth was born abroad as an American citizen) to expanding the college-educated workforce.[1]

Research on improving America's competitiveness also demonstrates the broader degree to which businesses are reliant on skilled immigrants in their workforces. In a survey of Harvard Business School alumni, nearly one in four said that at least 15 percent of their companies' US-based skilled workforce was foreign-born.[2] Immigrants, they said, were critical for developing better products and services, increasing the quality of innovation, and reaching international customers. Over two-thirds reported that their companies' operations would be harmed if denied access to skilled foreign workers. In

Figure 1. Migration of Inventors, 2000–2010

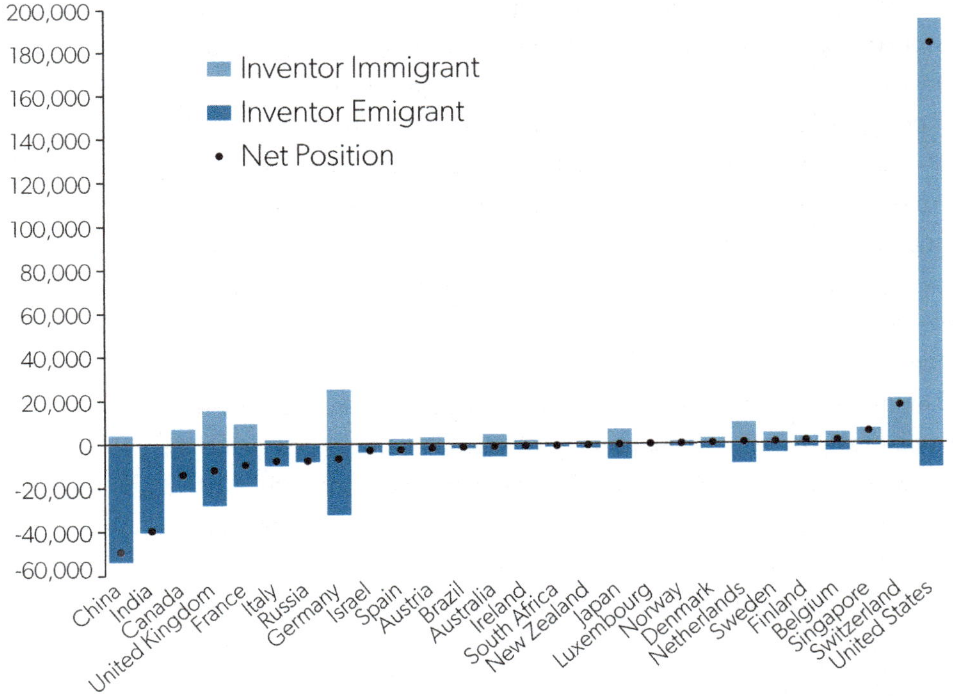

Source: Data from Ernest Miguelez and Carsten Fink, "Measuring the International Mobility of Inventors: A New Database" (WIPO Economic Research Working Paper No. 8, World Intellectual Property Organization, Geneva, Switzerland, 2013).

fact, nearly 60 percent already blamed the antiquated US immigration system for causing project delays. Figure 2 shows the broad net agreement about skilled immigration between business leaders and the general public.[3]

Despite these contributions, there are calls to cease immigration programs like H-1B visas and Optional Practical Training (OPT). Those changes would come at a heavy price for American innovation. Our best companies rely on H-1B workers for hard-to-fill positions. The tech sector, a huge driver of economic growth and creator of American jobs, needs the skills these workers provide to develop their products and invent new technologies. The OPT program, meanwhile, allows us to take advantage of foreign students' willingness to contribute to our economy after they conclude their studies. International students help fund our educational institutions and academic research, enrich the learning environment for American students, and further the exchange of ideas. To break our promise of opportunity to these students would dampen the enthusiasm

Figure 2. Net Agreement for Belief Statements about Immigration

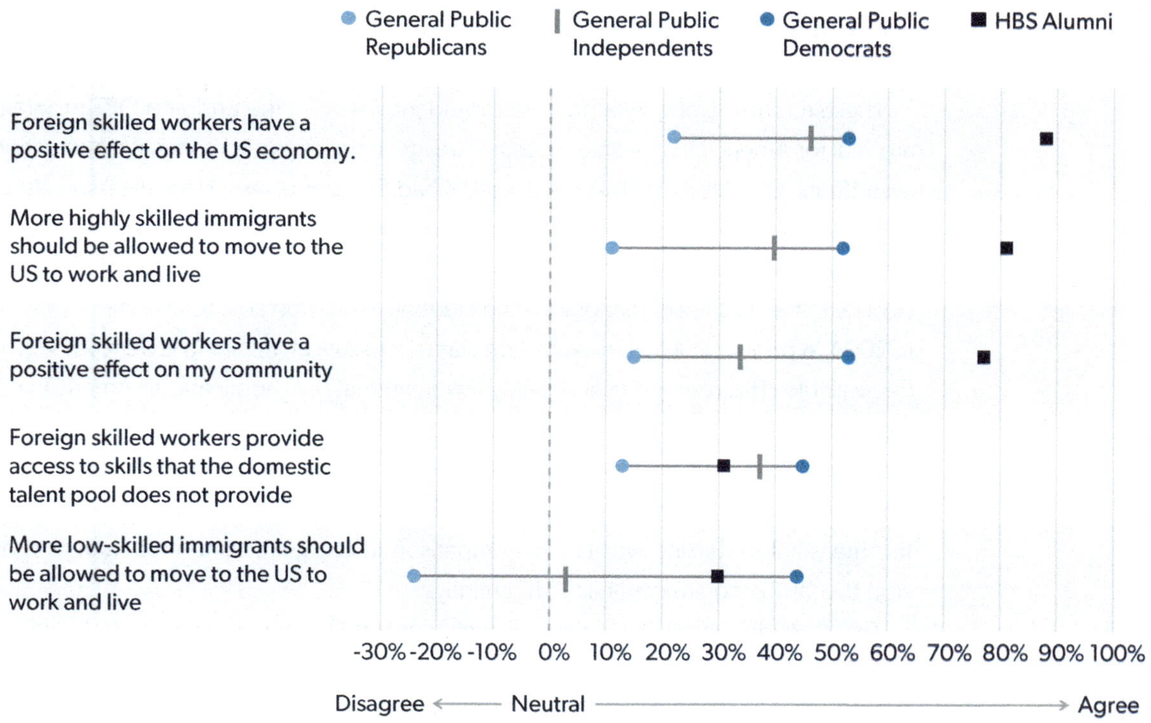

Note: Net agreement is calculated as the percentage of respondents who agree with the statement minus the percentage of respondents who disagree with the statement. Calculations exclude responses of "Don't know" and "Not applicable to me/my company."
Source: Michael E. Porter, Jan W. Rivkin, Mihir A. Desai, Katherine M. Gehl, William R. Kerr, and Manjari Raman, A Recovery Squandered: The State of U.S. Competitiveness 2019 (Boston, MA: Harvard Business School, 2019), https://www.hbs.edu/competitiveness/Documents/a-recovery-squandered.pdf.

of the world's youth to use and grow their talents here. In turn, it would weaken our economic competitiveness in the future.

Rather than end the programs, we should take the opportunity to make them stronger. The H-1B visa, for example, is allocated through a very crude process. The US government received about 275,000 applications for 85,000 available visas in March 2020 (notably, after COVID-19 became prominent). But rather than prioritize the highest-value uses of this scarce supply of visas, the government allocates them via two random lotteries—a loss for America as a whole. This crudeness can even result in uses of the program that hurt American workers. As an alternative, I have argued for wage ranking each company's visa applications.[4] This system would award visas to companies that will pay the most for each position; thus, visa distribution would be based on signals from the labor market—how much companies are willing to pay for talent—rather than on a randomized lottery. Whether through wage ranking, stricter H-1B minimum wages, visa auctions, or some other sensible measure, now is the time to start making the best use of available visas.

America has historically sat at the center of global talent exchanges, and it would be devastating to lose this special position.

These reforms, along with preserving student visas and the bridging OPT program, are vital for America to cultivate a positive image in the eyes of prospective international students. One study by Takao Kato and Chad Sparber gives a forceful lesson about how much foreign students, especially the best ones, consider future access to US jobs when choosing to come to college in America.[5] The researchers analyzed a modest decline in the likelihood that graduating students would be able to acquire H-1B visas in 2004. A prior visa program expansion was due to sunset, meaning fewer visas would be available. This resulted in noticeably fewer international applicants to American colleges, despite the fact that those potential students wouldn't even need H-1B visas until graduation, four or more years later. The choice of students to go elsewhere was especially pronounced among the most qualified candidates. The 2004 event that caused this measurable decline was tiny in comparison to today's calls to end student visas, stop the OPT program, and halt H-1B entirely.

This episode reveals the degree to which uncertainty can damage skilled immigration. The US immigration system has never been "user friendly," to be sure. The world's talent was willing to put up with the hurdles for the opportunity to study and work in America. This investment made our country a special place for innovation and invention (figure 1), and people are most willing to invest when they feel secure in the future. But hostile rhetoric and anti-immigration policy actions over the past few years have already dulled the luster of America for those abroad, causing deep uncertainty about investing in this country. Some graduate education fields like business schools have already witnessed two or three years of consecutive declines in foreign applications, over-and-above any changes in application rates from natives.[6] Closing the borders to stop the spread of the pandemic was the right choice; closing them unnecessarily into the future will place America on a new trajectory away from global talent that will be hard (or impossible) to reverse.

Even before COVID-19, other countries were increasingly competing with us to take more market share in the global talent market. For example, America's share of college-educated migrants is falling relative to other OECD countries.[7] Innovative programs in other nations to attract these future innovators further threaten our competitive advantage. America, too, must innovate.

One bipartisan opportunity for policy innovation is an immigrant entrepreneur visa.[8] Despite the many case studies of foreign entrepreneurs aiding America, our existing immigration pathways have an unfortunate gap when it comes to aspiring entrepreneurs who are not already wealthy. Thus, while we have programs that facilitate the migration of foreigners who can invest $1.8 million into a US business, we don't have a secure pathway for a graduating college student who has a strong business idea but little existing wealth. Given the desirability of the jobs created by new businesses—the ultimate free lunch, perhaps—countries like Australia, Canada, and the United Kingdom have each created their own entrepreneur visa. These programs have strong qualification standards (e.g., the entrepreneur's background, the economic impact their presence will achieve, etc.) and sometimes require that the entrepreneur has successfully raised start-up capital from qualified investors. Absent such a program in the United States, aspiring entrepreneurs either create awkward workarounds (e.g., work nights and weekends on the idea while on an H-1B visa) or go to another country. In recent years, more than two dozen bills have been introduced in Congress by Democrats and Republicans to remedy this weak spot and received bipartisan support, but we need to get one of these pushed through and enacted.

When it soon becomes time to fully reopen our borders to immigrants, let us be prepared to reform our immigration system to work better for all stakeholders.

When it soon becomes time to fully reopen our borders to immigrants, let us be prepared to reform our immigration system to work better for all stakeholders.[9] The Harvard Business School survey showed remarkable consistency across business leaders and the general public for wanting to bolster the employment-based nature of US admissions. While now is not the right time for designing and debating such extensive overhauls, policymakers can use this challenging environment to make some quick wins that provide momentum for when reform is feasible. Implementing a better H-1B visa allocation system and establishing a visa for immigrant entrepreneurs are two possibilities.

Above all, we must educate voters and build support for policies that enhance American innovation and American competitiveness. While blaming foreigners for economic or public health troubles has long been part of the nationalism playbook, economic integration and openness to foreign talent are a stronger path for long-term success as a country.

William Kerr is the D'Arbeloff Professor of Business Administration at Harvard Business School.

Endnotes

1 William R. Kerr, *The Gift of Global Talent: How Migration Shapes Business, Economy & Society* (Stanford, CA: Stanford Business Books, 2019).

2 Michael E. Porter, Jan W. Rivkin, Mihir A. Desai, Katherine M. Gehl, William R. Kerr, and Manjari Raman, *A Recovery Squandered: The State of US Competitiveness 2019* (Boston, MA: Harvard Business School, 2019), https://www.hbs.edu/competitiveness/Documents/a-recovery-squandered.pdf.

3 Ibid., 50.

4 Kerr, "Gift of Global Talent."

5 Takao Kato and Chad Sparber, "Quotas and Quality: The Effect of H-1B Restrictions on the Pool of Prospective Undergraduate Students from Abroad," *Review of Economics and Statistics* 95, no. 1 (March 2013): 109–26, https://doi.org/10.1162/REST_a_00245.

6 Scott Jaschik, "Understanding the Decline in MBA Applications," *Inside Higher Ed*, February 4, 2019, https://www.insidehighered.com/admissions/article/2019/02/04/new-data-help-explain-decline-mba-applications.

7 Kerr, "Gift of Global Talent."

8 Sari Pekkala Kerr and William R. Kerr, "Immigration Policy Levers for US Innovation and Startups," in *Innovation and Public Policy*, ed. Austan Goolsbee and Benjamin Jones (Chicago: University of Chicago Press, forthcoming), https://www.hbs.edu/faculty/Publication%20Files/20-105_aac0d5ae-e6e3-4570-8225-31bcc127f693.pdf.

9 Ibid.

CHAPTER 2

Immigration as a Tool to Boost US Economic Growth and Prosperity

Pia M. Orrenius and Madeline Zavodny

As unemployment rates soar, policymakers may be tempted to try to protect American workers from perceived labor market competition from immigrants. Slamming the door shut to new immigrants and even making some current immigrants leave may seem like a sure-fire way to make more jobs available to laid-off American workers. But such moves would do little to create jobs in the short run and would prove counterproductive in the longer run.

Policymakers need to recognize that the labor market is not zero-sum. There is not a fixed number of jobs in the economy. Rather, the economic pie grows with more workers and with the capital that accompanies labor.

Foreign-born workers rarely take jobs away from US-born workers. Instead, most employers turn to immigrants when they are unable to find American workers with the needed skills or vocation. Immigrants in occupations where supply cannot otherwise increase fast enough to meet demand or in jobs that US natives eschew are complements to native-born workers. Many immigrants are in STEM occupations that are central to technological and medical innovation and spur investment in research and development. Immigrants create jobs for some US natives via those channels as well as by starting new companies and adding to aggregate demand. Decades of studies, summarized by the National Academies of Sciences, Engineering, and Medicine in 2017, provide little evidence that immigration harms US natives' employment.[1] Any adverse effects fall primarily on earlier immigrants, not US natives.

Policymakers need to recognize that... the economic pie grows with more workers and with the capital that accompanies labor.

As we argue in this essay, the US economy faces structural challenges that predate the COVID-19 pandemic. Immigration can help ameliorate these challenges. In the short run, there is little that immigration policy can do to help spur economic recovery. However, bad policy choices would slow down the recovery. In the longer run, well-designed immigration policy reform would help pave the way to faster economic growth and assist the government in paying off the massive bills that will eventually come due.

Short-Term Dynamics of Immigration and Growth

Immigration naturally slows during a recession. When employers stop hiring and wage growth stalls, there is less demand for and supply of foreign workers. With over 40 million jobless claims filed since March and the unemployment rate the highest it's been since the 1930s, immigrant inflows are likely to remain low in the near term. This makes it unnecessary for lawmakers to impose additional restrictions. Employers will be reluctant to incur the expense of sponsoring foreign workers for temporary visas or permanent residence when equally qualified American workers are readily available.

In some industries, however, domestic workers are not readily available, not even during a recession. In such cases, recession-induced immigration restrictions can be damaging. This extends beyond the limited exemptions to restrictions on temporary worker visas recently announced by the administration, namely H-2A agricultural visas and visas for COVID-19-related medical workers and researchers.

Immigrants are overrepresented in many sectors classified by the Department of Homeland Security as "critical infrastructure industries." These include not only relatively low-skilled farm workers and food processors but also relatively high-skilled workers in healthcare services and pharmaceutical industries. Preserving access to immigrant workers who are essential to these industries not only ensures that food, medical, and other supply chains remain intact during the economic downturn but also safeguards the companies that produce these goods and services as well as the jobs of the Americans they employ.

There is also little reason to impose additional restrictions on family-based immigration, which was already in sharp decline before the pandemic began. The number of newly arrived immigrants granted permanent residence on the basis of family ties fell by over 16 percent between fiscal years 2016 and 2018.[2] It's not clear whether would-be immigrants were deterred by tougher scrutiny of applications, perceptions of a more hostile climate toward immigrants, or other factors. Regardless, the downward trend was apparent even before the imposition of the new "public charge" rule, which will make it difficult for people without strong finances to receive permanent resident status.

Long-Term Outlook

The downward trend in immigration is troubling and points toward what could be a costly mistake by policymakers: imposing new rules that make the United States a less attractive place to potential immigrants for years to come. Even before the pandemic, the United States faced major long-term challenges, including an aging population, sluggish labor force and productivity growth rates, declining economic dynamism, and a growing federal debt. Immigration tends to reduce these problems and can have an even greater positive impact if policymakers prioritize reforms that would boost immigration's benefits.

Like many other industrialized countries, the United States faces a demographic ticking time bomb due to its aging population. The baby boomers are reaching retirement age, and birth rates are falling. While the United States has a large surplus of available workers right now because of the layoffs due to the pandemic, the underlying long-term trends are worrisome. The Congressional Budget Office (CBO) forecasts potential labor force growth of only 0.3 percent a year over the next decade.[3] The CBO lowered its forecasts for US employment and output growth even before the COVID-19 outbreak in part because of slower growth in the population and labor force. The fact that immigrants and their US-born children will make up all of the labor force growth over the next 15 years points to the essential role of immigrants in the economy.[4] New immigrants tend to be near the beginning of their careers, so admitting more of them, particularly on employment-based temporary or permanent visas, is a quick way to jump-start labor force growth. The country will need more immigrants, not fewer, once the economy recovers.

Immigrants, particularly highly skilled ones, are an important source of productivity growth, which also has been low by historical standards. Much of highly skilled immigrants' contribution to productivity growth is due to their disproportionate representation in STEM occupations and their higher rates of patenting and other innovative activities. Their tendency to settle in fast-growing urban areas also contributes to productivity growth via agglomeration economies. Immigration policies like the H-1B visa program, the optional practical training (OPT) program, and readily available international student visas have attracted those highly skilled immigrants to the United States and enabled many of them to stay here. Instead of making it harder for young adults to access these visas and programs, policymakers should create easier and wider pathways for student visa holders to transition to H-1B visas and then for H-1B visa holders to transition to permanent resident visas.

Immigration policy reform would help pave the way to faster economic growth and assist the government in paying off the massive bills that will eventually come due.

Internal migration and business formation rates have been falling in the United States for decades, signaling a less dynamic economy. The causes of both declines are unclear, but the implications are clearly bad for economic growth. Lower geographic mobility among workers constrains businesses' ability to expand their operations, and young businesses play a critical role in innovative activity, which in turn contributes to productivity growth. Immigrants, particularly new arrivals, help offset the trend of reduced dynamism since they tend to go to growing areas and start new businesses. Immigrants are twice as likely as US natives to start a business, and they found many of the high-tech businesses that are engines of economic growth.[5] Yet unlike Australia, Canada, New Zealand, and many European countries, the United States lacks an entrepreneur or business start-up visa program.

The national debt is high and growing. Federal debt held by the public exceeded $17 trillion before the pandemic, and now it's projected to end the fiscal year at nearly $21 trillion. The projected deficit for fiscal year 2020 more than tripled as a result of the pandemic. The United States is fortunate that the rest of the world has been willing to finance its debt at low interest rates. But the desire to hold US debt depends crucially on the strength of the US dollar, and is therefore subject to change. In addition, even at low interest rates, debt payments will take a growing share of the government's budget and result in a diminished capacity to spend on items such as healthcare, education, and infrastructure. Having a larger workforce would help repay the debt sooner, and stronger economic growth in the coming years would help even more. Increasing the number of foreign workers in the United States, particularly highly skilled ones, is a relatively easy way to achieve both higher net tax contributions and faster growth.

The United States should be a beacon of opportunity that welcomes talented, hard-working people, not one that closes its doors to foreigners.

The United States can best increase immigration's contribution to economic growth by prioritizing admission and retention of highly skilled immigrant workers, particularly those in STEM fields and healthcare. As we've advocated elsewhere, the best way to do this is to use auctions in place of the current first-come, first-served or random-lottery visa systems.[6] Auctioning permits that would allow employers to hire foreign workers would allocate visas to their highest-valued use and maximize immigration's economic impact. In addition, the United States should implement a program for entrepreneur or start-up visas to encourage innovative immigrants to come or stay here. Reversing the downward trend in international students would help ensure US employers have an adequate supply of highly skilled workers in the future as well as benefit cash-strapped US colleges and universities.[7]

The United States should be a beacon of opportunity that welcomes talented, hard-working people, not one that closes its doors to foreigners. Immigration is not a silver bullet that can solve all the challenges facing the US economy, but if managed sensibly, it can be part of the solution. Disrupting immigration in the short run may well harm or delay the recovery from the pandemic. In contrast, carefully crafted reforms will enable immigration to further boost economic growth and prosperity in the long run.

Pia M. Orrenius is Vice President in the Research Department of the Federal Reserve Bank of Dallas.

Madeline Zavodny is a professor of economics at the University of North Florida.

Endnotes

1 Francine D. Blau and Christopher Mackie, eds., *The Economic and Fiscal Consequences of Immigration* (Washington, DC: National Academies Press, 2017).

2 Department of Homeland Security, "Table 6. Persons Obtaining Lawful Permanent Resident Status by Type and Major Class of Admission: Fiscal Years 2016 to 2018," November 13, 2019, https://www.dhs.gov/immigration-statistics/yearbook/2018/table6.

3 Congressional Budget Office, *The Budget and Economic Outlook: 2020 to 2030*, January 28, 2020, https://www.cbo.gov/publication/56020/.

4 Jeffrey S. Passel and D'Vera Cohn, "Immigration Projected to Drive Growth in US Working-Age Population through at Least 2035," *Fact Tank*, Pew Research Center, March 8, 2017, https://www.pewresearch.org/fact-tank/2017/03/08/immigration-projected-to-drive-growth-in-u-s-working-age-population-through-at-least-2035/.

5 Robert W. Fairlie, "Open for Business: How Immigrants Are Driving Small Business Creation in the United States," New American Economy, August 14, 2012, https://research.newamericaneconomy.org/report/open-for-business-how-immigrants-are-driving-small-business-creation-in-the-united-states-2/.

6 Pia Orrenius and Madeline Zavodny, "An Auctions Approach to Immigration Policy," Center for Growth and Opportunity at Utah State University, February 20, 2020, https://www.thecgo.org/research/an-auctions-approach-to-immigration-policy.

7 Pia Orrenius and Chloe Smith, "Without Immigration, US Economy Will Struggle to Grow," *Dallas Fed Economics*, Federal Reserve Bank of Dallas, April 9, 2020, https://www.dallasfed.org/research/economics/2020/0409.

CHAPTER 3

Immigrant Entrepreneurs: What Is Their Role in the Pandemic Recovery Effort?

Sari Pekkala Kerr

The COVID-19 pandemic has hit US households and businesses very hard. Particularly hard hit are small businesses, many of which have now been closed for months with minimal, if any, income or public support. The US small business sector is increasingly made up of immigrant-founded firms, which are particularly prevalent in COVID-19 hotspot locations in New York, New Jersey, California, and Florida.[1] As the US economy begins to reopen, what is the role of these immigrant-founded firms in the recovery effort? And what policies will make them more (or less) successful in bringing back the jobs to those hard-hit areas?

While making exact predictions in these highly uncertain times is impossible, we can draw from recent research to depict a reasonably well-informed view of the role of immigrant entrepreneurs in the US economy during the recovery phase in 2020 and beyond.

First, it is important to remember that the "entrepreneurial pool," the backbone of the small-business sector, has continually become more diverse over the last two decades. The shares of immigrant and female entrepreneurs have increased, along with the shares of Latino and Black owners, as well as the owners from ethnic backgrounds such as Mexican, Chinese, and Indian. New firm formation and job creation are currently much more dependent on these diverse entrepreneurs than they were in the 1990s and early 2000s.[2] More inclusive policies and programs may be warranted to reach this diverse group of entrepreneurs. One example of such is the State Small Business Credit Initiative (SSBCI) that was created as part of the Small Business Jobs Act of 2010, with a specific objective to expand access to credit to businesses in low- and moderate-income areas, and in minority and other underserved communities.

Immigrant entrepreneurs... create roughly one in four of all jobs in those young firms,

Second, immigrant entrepreneurs alone are responsible for a lot of new hiring among young firms. They create roughly one in four of all jobs in those young firms, but the share increases to 40 percent and above in places such as Silicon Valley, New York City, and other tech hubs. This is significant given that young firms are responsible for a disproportionate number of newly created jobs, and many major drivers of our economy develop in those firm cohorts.[3] Ensuring the viability of already existing young firms is critical if we want them to continue their role as job creation engines. Likewise, fostering an environment for firm birth (whether immigrant-founded or otherwise) helps to make the recovery more robust in the medium to short run. During the recovery phase, this could, for example, include more broadly introducing programs such as the Self-Employment Assistance (SEA) programs that already exist in five states to enable unemployed workers to start their own businesses that create jobs for themselves and others.[4]

Figure 1. Shares of Self-Employed Women, Immigrants, Blacks, and Hispanics (2001–2018)

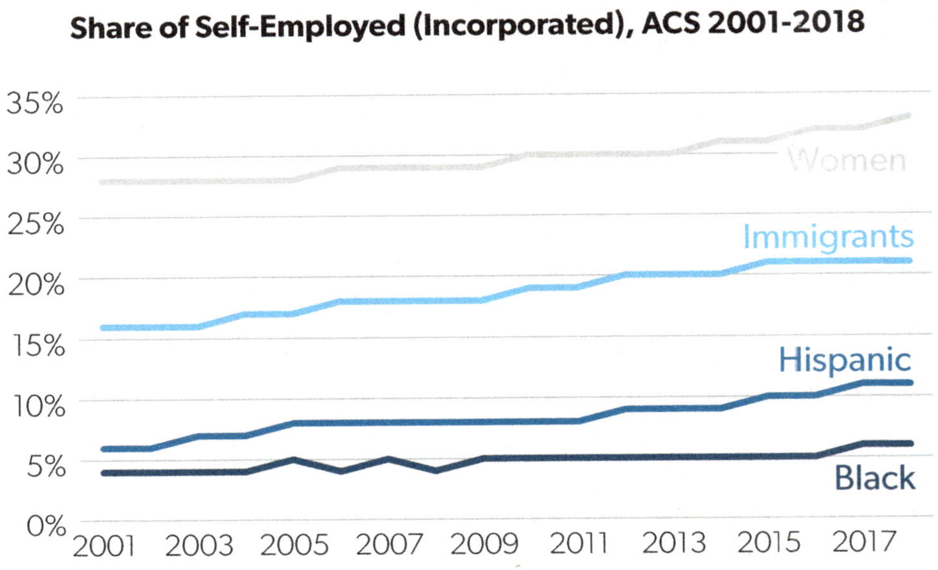

Source: Author calculations using American Community Survey IPUMS data, 2001-2017, IPUMS USA, University of Minnesota, www.ipums.org.

Third, immigrant-owned firms are particularly prevalent in the service sector (e.g., accommodation and food services, and other personal services), as well as many other sectors that were hardest hit by the pandemic.[5] Notably, the service sector establishments that are minority- or immigrant-owned tend to have the smallest amount of capital to survive any extended closures or other shocks. These firms, once open, offer a dependable stream of employment given the very labor-intensive nature of the business. It is, therefore, essential to ensure that these firms can reopen successfully; otherwise, many of the jobs we have relied upon will be lost. The issues that may need solving include, among others, delayed rental and tax payments, expired licenses, and any inspections required to reopen with state-mandated COVID-specific safety measures. For example, a natural solution to the backlog in licensing would be to extend all existing licenses for 12 months and focus efforts on enforcing the COVID-19 related regulations. In general, immigrants struggle more with occupational licensing in many areas, and additional assistance for non-native speakers is warranted during the recovery phase and beyond. These issues may be local in nature or may require more coordinated action at the state or federal levels.

It is likewise worth noting that many immigrant-founded firms are extremely dependent on being able to hire immigrant labor either through the skills-focused H1-B program, or through the various seasonal worker programs, as well as co-ethnic immigrants who are already in the country, either naturalized or on various work visas or green cards.[6] When firms reopen and are allowed to bring back their workers, it is critically important that immigration policies do not make it harder to re-employ this pool of labor. Many of the federal immigration programs were either halted or have become severely backlogged during the pandemic.

Compared to native-owned businesses, immigrant-owned firms are also more focused on exporting and other international activities. For such companies, much of their business income can be derived from that international channel.[7] When beginning to open up international travel and trade routes, it is crucial to make sure that policies do not undermine the ability of businesses to engage in the international markets.

In terms of already existing policies directly aimed at economic recovery from the COVID-19 crisis, it is unclear as to how much the immigrant-owned businesses have been able to benefit from the federal recovery effort and small business loans. Specifically, reports in many news outlets indicate that minority- and immigrant-owned businesses have been unable to participate in the Paycheck Protection Program (PPP) either due to some program requirements or simply because the program ran out of money before most of these small businesses were able to apply. In addition, program regulations are generally written in language that is not easily accessible to non-native English speakers. To make sure federal assistance is more broadly available, local officials who know their small business communities could consider, for example, offering consultation for applicants. These issues are worth investigating and rectifying, given the likelihood that these mostly small businesses will play a key role in the economic recovery and recreation of jobs.

Immigrants will have a major part in the economic recovery from the COVID-19 crisis.

In sum, the importance of immigrant entrepreneurs as firm founders and job creators has grown significantly over the last few decades. Immigrants will have a major part in the economic recovery from the COVID-19 crisis. The issues faced by immigrant-owned firms are the very same ones that native owners of small businesses struggle with. Yet they also have some specific concerns that could be addressed in order to ensure a successful reopening of existing firms and a launch of new immigrant-founded enterprises. US economic recovery will be much smoother if policymakers can readily respond to those needs at the local, state, and federal levels.

Sari Pekkala Kerr is an economist and a senior research scientist at the Wellesley Centers for Women at Wellesley College.

Endnotes

1 Sari Pekkala Kerr and William R. Kerr, "Immigrant Entrepreneurship in America: Evidence from the Survey of Business Owners 2007 & 2012," *Research Policy* 49, no. 3 (April 2020), https://doi.org/10.1016/j.respol.2019.103918.

2 Sari Pekkala Kerr and William R. Kerr, "Firms and Founders: Has the American Entrepreneur Changed over the Past Decades?" (working paper, 2020).

3 John C. Haltiwanger, Ron S. Jarmin, and Javier Miranda, "Who Creates Jobs? Small versus Large versus Young," *Review of Economics and Statistics* 95, no. 2 (2013): 347–61, https://doi.org/10.1162/REST_a_00288.

4 US Department of Labor, "Self-Employment Assistance," Employment and Training Administration, November 1, 2019, https://oui.doleta.gov/unemploy/self.asp#:~:text=Self%2DEmployment%20Assistance%20offers%20dislocated,starting%20their%20own%20small%20businesses; US Department of Labor, "Self-Employment Assistance (SEA)," fact sheet, May 1, 2020, https://oui.doleta.gov/unemploy/docs/factsheet/SEA_FactSheet.pdf.

5 Kerr and Kerr, "Immigrant Entrepreneurship."

6 Co-ethnic hiring varies greatly depending both on the ethnicity of the business founder as well as the local supply of co-ethnic labor. See: Sari Pekkala Kerr and William R. Kerr, "Whose Job Is It Anyway? Co-ethnic Hiring Patterns among Immigrant-Founded Firms in the United States" (working paper, 2020).

7 Kerr and Kerr, "Immigrant Entrepreneurship."

CHAPTER 4

Immigration is the Ultimate Security

Tim Kane

The state of human affairs became clearer in the year 2020: the thin veneer of law that sustains civil society was set ablaze in protest against injustice, and the illusion of calm security was torn away by global panic over the COVID-19 pandemic. There is a fragility to globalization, a newfound awareness of how easily the modern world can retreat from exuberant connectedness. It may be that the centuries-long industrial migration from country to city found its peak in 2020 and that the ultimate effect of the digital revolution will be to reverse the trend. People can now Zoom, e-mail, download, and share culture and ideas remotely, from their safe estates on the edges of smaller towns. What about migration between nations? What about refugees in an uneven world?

"What about it?" says the nationalist. The utmost duty of the government is national security, and in this new world, if immigration's economic benefits come at the cost of security, then it's no longer worth it.

The social shift in attitudes against globalization in 2020 is about more than immigration. Tourism, education, and business travelers outnumbered migrants roughly 100 to 1 in recent years, but borders have been sealed against all of them. As of this summer, 126 countries are completely closed to outsiders. Only returning citizens may enter. Another 64 are partially closed, leaving fewer than 30 countries with no travel restrictions. The second wave of COVID-19 infections is coming and will only harden this new reality.

Whether you or I or the top epidemiologist think these barriers make sense doesn't matter. This is a populist era, and people are terrified. Security first.

Rather than resist the priority given to security over other concerns, immigration advocates would do well to co-opt it for two reasons. The first is pragmatism. Lecturing the public that your ideals are more important than theirs is a losing argument. The second is that immigration benefits national security far more than it costs. Indeed, the main benefit of immigration is security. It's about time that immigration hawks align with openness as a security imperative.

Many conservatives are worried, and rightly so, that some foreigners who travel to the United States are terrorists. Twenty years on, the emotional resonance of the 9/11 attacks still holds the social imagination. It feeds an irrational fear of immigrants, a fear reinforced by the Boston Marathon bombing in 2013, the coordinated suicide bombings and shootings in Paris in 2015, the cargo truck rampage that killed 86 pedestrians in Nice, France, during the summer of 2016, and multiple vehicle and knifing rampages in London during the spring of 2017. Radical Islamic terrorism all. Unfortunately, these episodes obscure the much larger security advantages of immigration.

Consider the 9/11 attacks again. Those terrorists came into the country on student visas, not as migrants. Nearly 3,000 people were their victims, including 372 foreign citizens. Secretary of State Condoleezza Rice remarked during a fifth anniversary remembrance at the State Department that, "among the many innocent victims of September 11 were hundreds of citizens from over 90 countries," including Egypt, Israel, Vietnam, and China.

Among the American victims on 9/11, scores were naturalized citizens. There was Chin Sun Wells, born in South Korea in 1976, who played basketball and softball as an Oklahoma high schooler while working at the local Walmart before enlisting in the US Army in 1998. There was Sergeant First Class Jose Calderon-Olmedo from Puerto Rico, in his 20th year on active duty in the army, a man who served multiple tours of duty overseas. There was Dong Chul Lee, an immigrant from South Korea who came to the United States in 1968 to study computer science, later working for the National Security Agency for 14 years after a stint in the US Air Force. There was Amgen scientist Dora Marie Menchaca, researching medicines to treat cancer and pneumonia, wife and mother, killed at the age of 45 on her way home. Dora scribbled a note that was later recovered from the wreckage of American Airlines Flight 77, which crashed into the Pentagon: "Dear Earl, I love you. Please take care of Imani and Jaryd for me. Dora. 9/11/01 7:15 AM PST (I think)." She was born in Mexico and raised in Texas.

Immigrants did not attack America on 9/11. Rather, they were attacked.

Immigrants did not attack America on 9/11. Rather, they were attacked.

If People Are the Ultimate Resource

"They say that population is national power," wrote the editors of the *Korea Times* in 2011.[1] "Korea is heading toward a declining stage as it is one of the fastest aging societies with a low birth rate." Geographically isolated between its traditional rivals China and Japan, and incessantly poised for war with communist North Korea, the leaders in Seoul are acutely aware of the dangers of a relatively small population. Their concern typifies the classical understanding of power from the writings of Herodotus to Hans Morgenthau, defined in terms of resources. The modern scholar most respected for his analysis of power, Joseph S. Nye Jr. believes that the measurement of power will always prove somewhat elusive, yet it ultimately begins with resources: "population, territory, natural resources, economic size, military forces, political stability, among others."[2]

Mao Zedong said that "power grows out of the barrel of a gun" at the beginning of the Chinese Civil War in 1949. His full quote, it should be noted, is that "political power" grows from the gun, suggesting he realized there were other types of power than brute force. Yet Mao often observed that the Chinese people comprised "one-quarter of humanity." Contrary to concerns that excess density weakened the nation, he wrote in 1949: "Even if China's population multiplies many times, she is fully capable of finding a solution; the solution is production," adding that, "Of all things in the world, people are the most precious."[3]

Policymakers of today face the same question. The implications for choosing an open or a closed immigration approach will define America's size and strength in this century as much as any other policy. The options were made rather plain in a report published by the US Census in early 2020:

> "Higher international immigration over the next four decades would produce a faster growing, more diverse, and younger population for the United States. In contrast, an absence of migration into the country over this same period would result in a US population that is smaller than the present. Different levels of immigration between now and 2060 could change the projection of the population in that year by as much as 127 million people, with estimates ranging anywhere from 320 to 447 million US residents."[4]

Bravery and Brains

Brawn is only one of three strategic advantages that a nation of immigrants has over ethnically homogeneous powers. Bravery and brains are the other two.

Although skeptics worry that ethnic diversity yields a less unified and less patriotic people, history has proven the opposite time and time again. Of the soldiers in the US military during the Civil War (1861–1865), 43 percent were immigrants or the sons of immigrants, though only 13 percent of the total population of the North was foreign-born. In contrast, there were few migrant soldiers among the rebels. Why? The simple answer is that most immigration flows had been to northern states. There were more immigrants in 10 square miles of lower Manhattan than in over 770,000 square miles of the Confederacy.[5]

Not only did American immigrants volunteer for the military in disproportionately high numbers, but they were also awarded a disproportionately high number of medals. In the US military, the highest award for valor in action against an enemy is the Medal of Honor. In all, 1,522 Medals of Honor were awarded to soldiers and sailors who served during the Civil War; 369 of them were awarded to immigrants, mostly from Ireland and Germany.

When the United States entered World War I, 1.7 million foreign-born "aliens" registered for the draft. Military historians Alexander Barnes and Peter Belmonte estimate that 800,000 immigrants served in the army during the war. All told, 18 percent of the

American military in World War I was foreign-born, although only 14 percent of the total US population was.

The Pentagon today is acutely aware of the critical value of its immigrant servicemembers. Military leaders do not passively wait for foreign-born citizens to volunteer but follow the founding tradition of welcoming foreign citizens to enter the ranks. More than 760,000 noncitizens have enlisted and obtained US citizenship in the past century. Eastern Europeans were actively recruited between 1950 and 1959 thanks to the Lodge Act, designed to help gain an advantage if NATO came to blows with the Warsaw Pact. Over 100,000 noncitizens have joined the ranks of the US military since the 9/11 attacks, and over 10,000 have joined since 2008 through a special program focused on recruiting particularly skilled individuals through the Military Accessions Vital to the National Interest (MAVNI) program.

As for brains, the immigrant advantage is stark when it comes to Nobel Prizes, patents, and start-up companies. In every category, naturalized citizens are disproportionately adding more to the US economy than native-born citizens.

In 2015, five out of the nine US Nobel Prize recipients were living outside of their country of birth, and in 2014, four out of nine US recipients were immigrants. The story of Nobel Prize-winning immigrants is, in fact, an excellent proxy for the long history of the migration of talent to the United States. Foreign-born actors and performers, professional athletes, leaders in business and technology, and even noteworthy politicians migrate to the United States in droves to enrich their careers. Yet the dominance of immigrants at the 2016 Nobel Prize ceremony stands out. In that year, all six of the US Nobel recipients in the hard sciences were foreign-born.

No story could make the impact clearer than that of Albert Einstein, one of the thousands of Jewish people who fled Europe and ultimately helped the Allies develop the atomic bomb. In April 1933, Hitler's regime passed the first anti-Jewish ordinance that stripped one-quarter of Germany's physicists from their jobs. "The Jew wants to create contradictions everywhere and to separate relations, so that preferably, the poor naïve German can no longer make any sense of it whatsoever," wrote physicist Philipp Lenard, an earlier German recipient of the Nobel Prize and leader of the Deutsche Physik movement in the 1930s; Lenard claimed Einstein's theories of relativity were a corruption. The Nazi regime embodied the polar opposite of ethnic diversity that the United States represents. Einstein could have migrated anywhere, but he chose the United States.

The facts do point to the unavoidable conclusion that national security will be enhanced by greater, not less, immigration.

In 1939, a year before he would pass his American citizenship test, Einstein wrote a letter to President Roosevelt detailing the capabilities of a potential nuclear bomb, warning that Germany could be in the process of developing their own such weapon, and urging the United States to adopt a nuclear program. This famous letter prompted the Manhattan Project.[6] Then, following the war, the White House authorized a military operation to recruit thousands of German rocket scientists, even those with Nazi backgrounds, in order to gain a research advantage over Soviet Russia. Similarly, today, the United States is in a "brains race" for talent in the field of artificial intelligence and may already have more Chinese-born scientists than Beijing has. Can the nation afford to lose that race?

Increased Immigration Improves National Security

These are the facts. Having the facts on your side doesn't mean you will win the argument, of course. But the facts do point to the unavoidable conclusion that national security will be enhanced by greater, not less, immigration. COVID-19 has let loose an irrational fear of foreigners in all countries, causing an abrupt collapse in globalization that may become permanent. And yet this strange time offers an opportunity. The United States will become stronger than ever, and far stronger than China, by embracing its heritage of exceptional openness.

Tim Kane is the JP Conte Fellow in Immigration Studies at the Hoover Institution at Stanford University where he specializes in economic growth, immigration, and national security. Parts of this essay are excerpted from his forthcoming book, The Immigrant Superpower (Oxford University Press).

Endnotes

1 Editorial, "Population Is National Power," *Korea Times*, May 31, 2011, http://www.koreatimes.co.kr/www/news/opinon/2013/08/202_88043.html#.

2 Joseph S. Nye Jr., "Soft Power," *Foreign Policy*, no. 80 (Autumn 1990): 178, https://www.jstor.org/stable/1148580.

3 Xing Lu, *The Rhetoric of Mao Zedong: Transforming China and Its People* (Columbia: University of South Carolina Press, 2017), 2.

4 Sandra Johnson, *A Changing Nation: Population Projections under Alternative Immigration Scenarios* (Washington, DC: US Census Bureau, February 2020), https://www.census.gov/content/dam/Census/library/publications/2020/demo/p25-1146.pdf.

5 Tyler Anbinder, *City of Dreams: The 400-Year Epic History of Immigrant New York* (Boston, MA: Houghton Mifflin Harcourt, 2016), 207.

6 US Department of Energy, "Einstein's Letter," The Manhattan Project, an Interactive History, accessed June 19, 2020, https://www.osti.gov/opennet/manhattan-project-history/Events/1939-1942/einstein_letter.htm.

CHAPTER 5

How Immigrants Can Help the "Transition to a Great Economy" after COVID-19

Giovanni Peri

The Risk of Negative Post-COVID-19 Attitudes on Immigration

The impact of the COVID-19 pandemic in the US has been pervasive and extreme. It has caused a death toll higher than 100,000 (as of May 27, 2020) and it has ushered in an economic contraction with the unemployment rate at 15 percent nationally (as of April 2020) and a decline of US gross domestic product by 4.8 percent just in the first quarter of 2020. Families have been left struggling and in economic hardships. The mental, human, and social consequences of the lockdown and of social isolation have been deep. Many small businesses have been struggling to survive. Entire communities have been brought to the verge of collapse by a healthcare crisis that has overextended hospitals and exhausted healthcare workers.

Besides these material changes, the pandemic has also brought insidious changes in people's attitudes. The fear of a virus that originated namely from China has increased the hostility toward Chinese, Chinese-Americans, and immigrants in general.[1] Moreover, in times of crisis and economic uncertainty, the temptation to find scapegoats is very high. Immigrants have typically been targeted in such times as a group that is easy to identify and blame.[2]

Fueling these feelings, on April 22, President Donald J. Trump announced in a tweet an "Executive Order to temporarily suspend immigration into the United States!" to protect "the jobs of our GREAT American Citizens." On April 24, he signed Executive Order 10014, which, albeit filled with qualifications, halted for two months the issuing of residence permits (green cards) to people who wanted to immigrate to the United States. While this measure in the short run will not affect too many people (as very few are attempting to move to the United States during the pandemic), it is damaging as it strengthens the insidious and incorrect sentiment that immigrants are hurting the US economy and US workers. It also reveals that the current administration is using the pandemic to carry even further their restrictive immigration agenda. Other immigration restrictions may be on the way.

Executive Order 10014 is in line with several actions of the current administration aimed at reducing, slowing, and complicating legal immigration, while at the same time doubling down on enforcement and the deportation of undocumented immigrants. Previous executive orders banned immigration from some countries deemed a risk of terrorism, which mostly affected students and the highly educated from those areas. The number of F-1 student visas issued has been declining in each of the last three years.[3] There has been no policy or action to relax the very strict limit on skilled-immigrants visas (H1-B) in spite of the large demand for them exceeding the quota each year since 2014.[4]

What is most discouraging about these policies is that the president regularly claims their rationale to be a benefit for US workers and for the US economy. In what follows, I argue that such a vision is based on an erroneous understanding of the working of the US economy. In place of closing America's borders, I will explain why more open immigration policies should be an essential part of the recovery during the economic reopening.

The Fallacy of Restricting Immigration

Both before and after the COVID crisis, the economic reasoning used to justify immigration restrictions has been that halting immigration would help Americans get jobs. Let me state in very simple terms that such a view is not founded on economic analysis or evidence. In fact, it denotes a lack of familiarity with the economic analysis of immigration. The idea is based on an oversimplification that obscures understanding of the actual economic effects of immigrants.

Within a very simple model of demand and supply of homogeneous workers in one local labor market, with all other things fixed and when immigrants supply only labor, an inflow of immigrants would reduce wages or displace some of the existing workers. No reasonable economist, however, would think that such a simplistic model, used simply to illustrate a potential competition effect, is a good representation of what happens to a complex economy like the United States, when a differentiated group of individuals, like immigrants, joins it.

First, immigrants are not only workers but also consumers. Immigrants demand goods and services, increasing the demand for additional workers.[5] Second, immigrants are also entrepreneurs at a higher rate than natives, and as such, they create new firms and produce new jobs.[6] Third, they are a highly differentiated group, with innovators and scientists who improve firms' productivity and stimulate job creation, and also manual workers who specialize in jobs that US citizens are vacating.[7] The United States should definitely encourage some of these individuals, who stimulate the US economy and complement US workers' abilities, to come to the United States during the recovery after the COVID-19 crisis and help create a virtuous economic cycle.

Moreover, there is abundant evidence that many parts of the economy promptly respond to the inflow of immigrants, magnifying their positive effect. Firms invest more to take advantage of new workers, and they adjust and improve technology.[8] Trade is stimulated by the international links brought by immigrants.[9] All these factors contribute to grow the economy and to add jobs, and they have been shown to be quantitatively important by extensive economics research in the last 15 years.[10] In aggregate, immi-

Figure 1. Percentage of Immigrants in Essential Industries

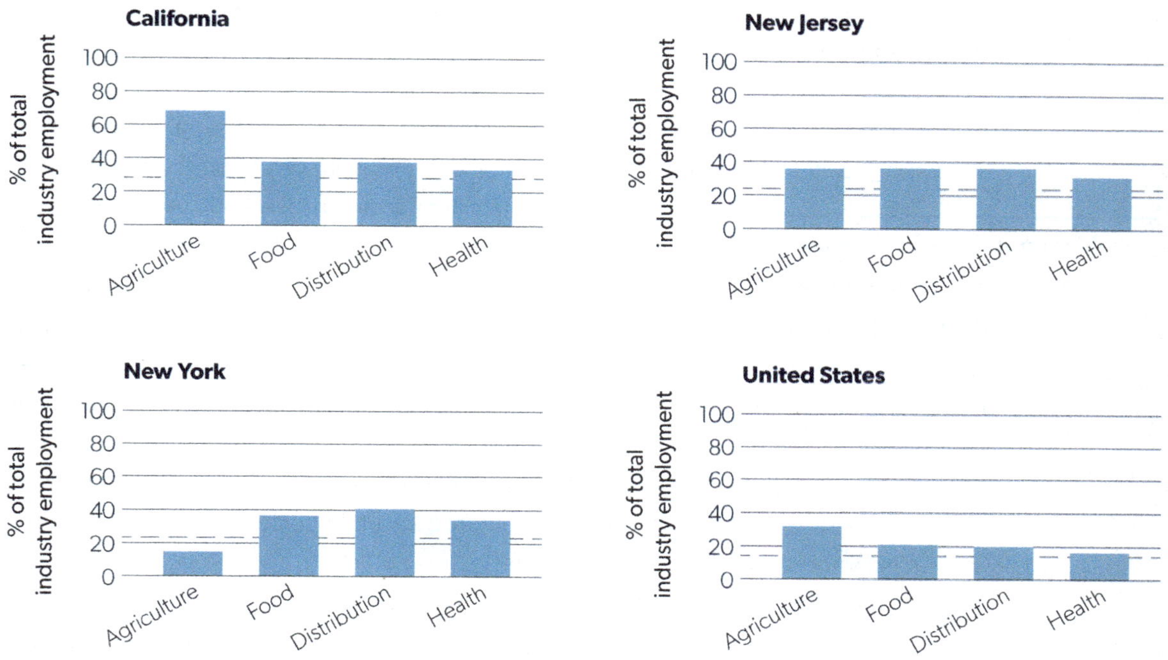

Source: Author's calculations using American Community Survey data, 2018.

gration does not hurt the employment and wages of natives, as these mechanisms completely reverse the pure competition effect described in the simple model.[11]

The massive current unemployment rate of Americans is generated by decreased demand for labor due to the fact that people and businesses are limited in their interactions, and because uncertainty about reopening is substantial. As a consequence of this, immigration has also come to a standstill. However, when businesses open their doors again, the roles of immigrants, as entrepreneurs, innovators, scientists, consumers, and workers, will help American workers to get back on track. Immigrants will again contribute to the growth of the US economy.

Recognizing the Economic Relevance of Immigrants and Promoting Growth

An additional reason for implementing policies reversing the decline in immigration, which has happened for the last decade in the United States, is the recognition, brought by COVID-19, of the essential role of immigrants during the crisis.[12] In the United States as a whole, as well as in the largest and most affected states (California and, even more, New York and New Jersey), immigrants were significantly over-represented among four groups of workers that were considered "essential" during the pandemics and continued to work.

Considering the four sectors of "agriculture," "food processing," "distribution," and "healthcare" as "essential," figure 1 shows the share of foreign-born workers.[13] In all but the agricultural sector in New York, each is above the dashed line that represents the share of immigrants in the population of that jurisdiction. Focusing on health workers—many of whom were essential and at-risk workers during this pandemic—and looking at the most affected states of New York and New Jersey, where these workers were exposed to the most extreme risk, we see that close to one-third of them are foreign-born. While foreign-born workers constitute only 14 percent of the overall population in the United States, they comprise about 35 percent of healthcare workers in New York and 31 percent in New Jersey.

More open immigration policies should be an essential part of the recovery during the economic reopening.

Turning to agriculture, the US national production of agricultural goods depends heavily on foreign-born workers, who represent one-third of national workers and close to 70 percent of California's agricultural workers. Overall, it is indisputable that immigrants are a large and over-represented proportion of the group of essential workers in the United States. They are essential to the movement of food supplies from farms to grocery stores, and ultimately, to our kitchen tables.

Hence, in the light of their important role during the pandemic and their potential role in stimulating growth at the reopening of the economy, it would be wise to consider policies that open rather than close our immigration system. It will not be easy to attract immigrants to the United States after this health crisis. Certainly, it will take an inversion of current policy. Some simple policy suggestions are the following:

- Simplify access to permanent residence for foreign-born healthcare workers who have been working during the pandemic.
- Convert temporary visas into permanent residence or allow a path to legalization for workers who were in essential sectors and worked during the pandemic.
- Expand the H-1B skilled visa program, which helps create high tech jobs, which in turn have strong positive effects on local economies.
- Facilitate the enrollment of international students and increase the number of F-1 visas to reduce and reverse their steep decline.

Conclusion

Immigration has been declining in the United States for the past 20 years.[14] In part, this was because of the large decline in immigration from Mexico as well as the effects of restrictive and obsolete immigration policies. During the last four years, this restrictive tendency has accelerated, and immigration has declined even further. COVID-19 risks are generating fear and uncertainty, which may trigger further aversion to immigration and even more restrictive policies. As scholars, we need to make sure that solid economic research, rather than prejudice and a caricature of economic analysis, is part of the considerations in deciding immigration policies for the growth of the US economy during the transition out of the crisis.

Giovanni Peri is a professor of Economics and Director of the Global Migration Center at UC Davis.

Endnotes

1 Paula Larsson, "Anti-Asian Racism during Coronavirus: How the Language of Disease Produces Hate and Violence," The Conversation, March 31, 2020, https://theconversation.com/anti-asian-racism-during-coronavirus-how-the-language-of-disease-produces-hate-and-violence-134496.

2 Neeraj Kaushal, *Blaming Immigrants: Nationalism and the Economics of Global Movement* (New York: Columbia University Press, 2019).

3 Elizabeth Redden, "International Student Numbers in US Decline," *Inside Higher Ed*, April 23, 2019, https://www.insidehighered.com/quicktakes/2019/04/23/international-student-numbers-us-decline.

4 Youyou Zhou, "Winning the H-1B Visa Lottery Is No Longer Enough," *Quartz*, May 13, 2019, https://qz.com/1614743/winning-the-h-1b-visa-lottery-is-getting-more-and-more-difficult/.

5 Giovanni Peri, Derek Rury, and Justin C. Wiltshire, "The Economic Impact of Migrants from Hurricane Maria" (IZA Discussion Paper No. 13049, IZA Institute of Labor Economics, Bonn, Germany, March 2020), https://www.iza.org/publications/dp/13049/the-economic-impact-of-migrants-from-hurricane-maria.

6 Robert W. Fairlie and Magnus Lofstrom, "Immigration and Entrepreneurship," in *Handbook of the Economics of International Migration*, ed. Barry Chiswick and Paul Miller, vol. 1, (Amsterdam: Elsevier, North Holland, 2014), 877–911; Giovanni Peri, Kevin Shih, and Chad Sparber, "STEM Workers, H-1B Visas, and Productivity in US Cities," *Journal of Labor Economics* 33, no. 1 (2015): S225–S255; Giovanni Peri, "The Effect of Immigrants on US Employment and Productivity," *Federal Reserve Bank of San Francisco Economic Letter*, August 30, 2010, https://www.frbsf.org/economic-research/files/el2010-26.pdf.

7 William W. Olney, "Immigration and Firm Expansion," *Journal of Regional Science* 53, no. 1 (October 2013): 142–57, https://doi.org/10.1111/jors.12004.

8 Giovanni Peri and Francisco Requena Silvente, "The Trade Creation Effect of Immigrants: Evidence from the Remarkable Case of Spain," *Canadian Journal of Economics* 43, no. 4 (November 2010): 1433–59, https://www.jstor.org/stable/40925283.

9 Giovanni Peri, "Should the US Expand Immigration?," *Journal of Policy Analysis and Management* 39, no. 1 (Winter 2020): 267–74, https://doi.org/10.1002/pam.22185.

10 Giovanni Peri, "Do Immigrant Workers Depress the Wages of Native Workers?" *IZA World of Labor*, May 2014, https://wol.iza.org/articles/do-immigrant-workers-depress-the-wages-of-native-workers/long; Giovanni Peri, "Immigrants, Productivity, and Labor Markets," *Journal of Economic Perspectives* 30, no. 4 (2016): 3–30.

11 Giovanni Peri, "20 Years of Declining Immigration and the Disappearance of Low-Skilled Immigrants," *Immigration Facts*, UC Davis Global Migration Center, February 24, 2020, https://globalmigration.ucdavis.edu/20-years-declining-immigration-and-disappearance-low-skilled-immigrants.

12 For details on the sector definitions, see Giovanni Peri and Justin C. Wiltshire, "The Role of Immigrants as Essential Workers during the COVID-19 Pandemic," *Immigration Facts*, UC Davis Global Migration Center, April 27, 2020, https://globalmigration.ucdavis.edu/role-immigrants-essential-workers-during-covid-19-pandemic.

13 Source: Author's calculations using American Community Survey data, 2018.

14 Peri, "20 Years of Declining Immigration."

CHAPTER 6

Refugees and Asylum Seekers Can Help Us Rebuild after COVID-19

Margaret E. Peters

When we think of refugees and asylum seekers, we often think of destitute individuals who are fleeing war or other crises.[1] We also tend to think of these individuals as only needing help, not the extent to which they can help us. But those fleeing war, persecution, and other crises have long been an important part of American society and have greatly contributed to our economic growth. They can be an important part of our economy and society as we move forward from the COVID-19 crisis.

Refugees and asylum seekers are, by definition, in need of help when they come to the United States. In many cases they have had to flee their homes quickly, with little time to gather their belongings, let alone sell their property.[2] What little money they may have had will have likely been spent in transit. Refugees and asylum seekers, then, have to depend on governments and non-governmental organizations for assistance.[3]

We can be the generous "city upon a hill"—providing refugees with a chance to rebuild their lives— without fear that refugees and asylum seekers will harm our economic future.

In the US, refugees are eligible to receive a relatively large amount of assistance in their first year. This includes reception and placement grants to help them get settled, and cash, medical, and other assistance meant as a stopgap until they can find employment. Asylum seekers are not eligible for these benefits, or any other federal benefits, until they receive refugee status (although they may be eligible for state benefits). A recent report that was rejected by the Trump administration calculated that these benefits cost the government about $7,253.79 per refugee (including all family members) each year for the first 10 years they are in the country, or about $326.4 billion over 10 years.[4]

Yet the fact that refugees and asylum seekers come to our country with little and need government assistance does not mean that they do not make a contribution to our economy or society. That same government report found that refugees and their families contributed $343.3 billion in revenue over those same 10 years, for a net contribution of $16.9 billion.[5]

The fact that refugees and asylum seekers are net beneficiaries to the United States is not surprising to those who have studied them. Refugees and asylum seekers come to the United States not just for protection but also because they want to rebuild their lives. In a study of Syrian and Iraqi refugees, my co-authors and I found that refugees prioritized the ability to work when choosing a destination to settle in.[6] These refugees had suffered extreme amounts of violence at the hands of the Assad regime or the Islamic State. They had to flee quickly, usually leaving with only a few hours' or days' notice. In the process, they lost much of what may have given them a sense of self-worth: their jobs, their homes and other possessions, their communities, and for many, their family members or close friends. Refugees are often unmoored from all that defined them and now must make their way in a society that they don't know and maybe don't understand well. When asylum seekers flee their homes for a new country, the major goal for these migrants is safety, yes, but it is also to rebuild their lives. They want to get back what they lost: to build a new community and home.

The refugees and asylum seekers in our study saw work as one of the most important ways in which they could rebuild their lives. By working, they could take care of their family and be contributing members of society, regaining their status. And it's not just our respondents who feel this way; other studies have shown that refugees throughout the world move to where they can find jobs.[7]

This desire to rebuild their lives has meant that refugees and asylum seekers are great contributors to the US economy and American society.[8] We see this in places like Utica and other cities in Upstate New York, which have relied on refugees to help revive the economy and their towns by building businesses and community centers.[9]

Now, under COVID-19, refugees and asylum seekers are on the front lines as essential workers. They are doctors, nurses, and other healthcare workers;[10] they work in food processing, including 9,300 butchers and meat processors who work in an industry that has been badly hurt by COVID-19;[11] and they work in grocery stores.[12] They are also working in some of the hardest-hit regions—11,400 refugee healthcare workers are in New York—and in frontline positions—14.2 percent of refugee healthcare workers are registered nurses.[13]

As we consider reforms to our immigration system, we should not be using this time to push away the very people who are saving lives and revitalizing communities. Instead, we should continue to welcome refugees and asylum seekers. There are many policies and actions that can be taken in both the short and long run that will help ensure our economy grows and help rebuild our sense of community as the pandemic ends.

On the federal level, the Trump administration could immediately resettle more refugees. For fiscal year 2020 (October 1, 2019 through September 30, 2020), the Trump administration has set a ceiling of 18,000 refugees; historically we have resettled almost 80,000 refugees on average per year.[14] We should immediately increase the number of refugees resettled to at least the previous levels.

Additionally, we could shift our priorities in who is resettled. Currently, we cannot resettle all of those most in need of resettlement. One option is to prioritize those with prior experience in healthcare or other essential services. These individuals could be resettled in areas that have been the hardest hit by COVID-19. That way, they could immediately aid in the recovery for these communities.

We could also work to fix our broken asylum system. The asylum system has long faced backlogs,[15] and the Trump administration's "Remain in Mexico" program and other changes have led to increased violence and insecurity for the asylum seekers[16] but have not had a proven deterrent effect.[17] Instead of placing quotas on immigration judges,[18] we need to direct more resources to the border to adjudicate the asylum seekers' cases properly. We can also better ensure that asylum seekers are able to contribute to society if we adjudicate their cases more quickly. Studies have shown that the longer a refugee waits to join the labor market, the less likely he or she is to be employed in the future.[19] By providing status for asylum seekers quickly, they can begin working and rebuilding their lives.

Even without federal action, there are actions that states and localities can take. On the state level, many jobs require licensing before they can be done. These licensing requirements are often formidable burdens that can prevent immigrants from using their skills.[20] States could reform these licensing requirements to allow refugees and asylum seekers to use the skills they developed elsewhere. Additionally, states, localities, and civil society groups could invest more in English language programs, skills training programs, and programs that match refugees and asylum seekers to jobs that use their skills.

It has long been a part of the American creed to welcome those who are "yearning to be free," from some of the earliest settlers who fled religious persecution to those fleeing Communism during the Cold War to those fleeing war and persecution today. Some of these refugees, like Albert Einstein, become known for their major contributions to American society, but most live ordinary lives. Nonetheless, these refugees have long made significant contributions to our economy and our society. We can be the generous "city upon a hill"—providing refugees with physical safety and the social safety net programs, including access to jobs and healthcare, that give them a chance to rebuild their lives— without fear that refugees and asylum seekers will harm our economic future.

Margaret E. Peters is an associate professor in the Department of Political Science at UCLA.

Endnotes

1 Legal refugees are people fleeing a well-founded fear of persecution due to race, membership in a particular social group, political opinion, religion, or national origin. Asylum seekers are individuals who claim refugee status but have not yet been granted refugee status. There are other groups, like those living under temporary protected status and victims of human trafficking, who are granted a legal status but not all the rights and access to benefits that legal refugees receive.

2 Margaret E. Peters, Thania Sanchez, and Yang-Yang Zhou, "The Dignity of Forced Migrants: Explaining Migrants Destination Preferences" (working paper, UCLA, 2020.

3 For a primer on resettlement, see United Nations High Commissioner for Refugees, "Resettlement in the United States," UNHCR, March 2020, https://www.unhcr.org/resettlement-in-the-united-states.html; International Rescue Committee, "How the US Refugee Vetting and Resettlement Process Really Works," Rescue.org, last updated December 2, 2019, https://www.rescue.org/article/how-us-refugee-vetting-and-resettlement-process-really-works.

4 US Department of Health and Human Services, *The Fiscal Costs of the US Refugee Admissions Program at the Federal, State, and Local Levels, from 2005–2014* (draft), July 29, 2017, https://assets.documentcloud.org/documents/4056060/Refugee-Report-Draft.pdf.

5 Ibid.

6 Peters, Sanchez, and Zhou, "Dignity of Forced Migrants."

7 Christopher W. Blair, Guy Grossman, and Jeremy M. Weinstein, "Forced Displacement and Asylum Policy in the Developing World" (working paper, University of Pennsylvania, 2019); Nadwa Mossad, Jeremy Ferwerda, Duncan Lawrence, Jeremy M. Weinstein, and Jens Hainmueller, "In Search of Opportunity and Community: The Secondary Migration of Refugees in the United States" (working paper, 2019), https://ssrn.com/abstract=3458711.

8 Danny Bahar, "Why Accepting Refugees Is a Win-Win-Win Formula," *Up Front* (blog), Brookings, June 19, 2018, https://www.brookings.edu/blog/up-front/2018/06/19/refugees-are-a-win-win-win-formula-for-economic-development/; Amy Maxmen, "Migrants and Refugees Are Good for Economies," *Nature*, June 21, 2018, https://www.nature.com/articles/d41586-018-05507-0.

9 Christina Goldbaum, "Luring Refugees: NY Cities Desperate for People Try a New Strategy," *New York Times*, May 13, 2019, https://www.nytimes.com/2019/05/13/nyregion/refugees-upstate-ny-employment.html.

10 Filippo Grandi, "Refugees Are on the Front Line of the COVID-19 Pandemic. Let's Give Them the Rights They Deserve," World Economic Forum, April 30, 2020, https://www.weforum.org/agenda/2020/04/meet-the-asylum-seekers-on-the-frontline-of-the-coronavirus/; "Refugee Workers on the Frontlines and as Essential Workers," New American Economy, April 23, 2020, https://research.newamericaneconomy.org/report/refugee-on-the-frontlines-covid-19/.

11 NAE, "Refugee Workers on the Frontlines."

12 Ibid.

13 Ibid.

14 Migration Policy Institute, "US Annual Refugee Resettlement Ceilings and Number of Refugees Admitted, 1980–Present," March 2020, https://www.migrationpolicy.org/programs/data-hub/charts/us-annual-refugee-resettlement-ceilings-and-number-refugees-admitted-united.

15 Doris Meissner, Faye Hipsman, and T. Alexander Aleinikoff, "The US Asylum System in Crisis: Charting a Way Forward," Migration Policy Institute, September 2018, https://www.migrationpolicy.org/research/us-asylum-system-crisis-charting-way-forward.

16 Michael Garcia Bochenek, "US: 'Remain in Mexico' Program Harming Children," Human Rights Watch, February 12, 2020, https://www.hrw.org/news/2020/02/12/us-remain-mexico-program-harming-children.

17 In earlier research, scholars have found little effect of increased border enforcement on decisions to migrate. This is likely to be the case with the asylum seekers as they are fleeing not just poor economic

conditions but also violence. See, for example, Wayne A. Cornelius and Idean Salehyan, "Does Border Enforcement Deter Unauthorized Immigration? The Case of Mexican Migration to the United States of America," *Regulation & Governance* 1, no. 2 (May 2007): 139–53.

18 Joel Rose, "Justice Department Rolls Out Quotas for Immigration Judges," *National Public Radio*, April 3, 2018, https://www.npr.org/2018/04/03/599158232/justice-department-rolls-out-quotas-for-immigration-judges.

19 Jens Hainmueller, Dominik Hangartner, and Duncan Lawrence, "Lives on Hold," Immigration Policy Lab, 2016, https://immigrationlab.org/project/lives-on-hold-how-asylum-wait-times-impact-employment/; Moritz Marbach, Jens Hainmueller, and Dominik Hangartner, "The High Cost of Refugee Employment Bans," Immigration Policy Lab, 2018, https://immigrationlab.org/project/high-cost-of-refugee-employment-bans/.

20 Brenton D. Peterson, Sonal S. Pandya, and David Leblang, "Doctors with Borders: Occupational Licensing as an Implicit Barrier to High-Skill Migration," *Public Choice* 160, no. 1-2 (January 2014): 45–63, https://doi.org/10.1007/s11127-014-0152-8.

CHAPTER 7

The Case for Economic Openness in the Time of Coronavirus

Kimberly A. Clausing

After decades of increased income inequality and slow or stagnant wage growth, many Americans have concluded that the economy no longer works for them.[1] Sadly, these views are well-supported by economic statistics that show a divergence between growth in national income—which remains quite strong—and growth in the income of a typical household—which is far flatter.[2] These trends have only exasperated other types of inequality across groups, including the racial disparities that have driven recent protests.

The coronavirus crisis has placed inequality in a particularly harsh light, as the poor and vulnerable have been far more likely to suffer illness and death, and far more likely to face job loss and economic adversity.[3] And, while the early economic policy responses of both the Federal Reserve and Congress have been laudable, policymakers will need to be equally bold in the months ahead to avoid a long period of slow economic growth or stagnation.[4]

Unfortunately, the present crisis has also made isolationist economic policies look more attractive than they truly are.[5] Barriers to trade and immigration will only make a bad situation worse; there are far more effective ways to generate broad prosperity and inclusive economic growth.

Consider first trade barriers. It is undeniably true that the swift expansion of trade with poorer countries in recent decades generated important sources of disruption for many US workers.[6] Still, many other factors also contributed to such disruption: rapid technological progress that shifted labor demand away from those whose labor was most easily replaced by computerization or automation, a rise in the market power of large companies in many sectors of our economy, a decline in private sector unionization, changes in norms, and changes in economic policy that failed to counter, and at times exasperated, other sources of economic inequality.[7]

Barriers to trade and immigration will only make a bad situation worse; there are far more effective ways to generate broad prosperity and inclusive economic growth.

Since trade is part of the source of worker disruption, that makes trade barriers a tempting solution. Yet most of the time, trade barriers hurt the very people they purport to help. First, tariffs—or taxes on imports—are best understood as a regressive consumption tax.[8] Since the poor consume a higher fraction of their income and buy more imported products as a share of their total consumption, they also pay a higher share of their income in tariff costs. The research shows tariffs harming consumers time and again.[9] Second, as the last three years have made perfectly clear, our trading partners do not sit on their hands when we raise trade barriers on their exports.[10] They respond with tariffs of their own, and that hurts the many American workers whose jobs depend on exports, or access to imports.[11]

Third, tariffs harm our ability to work harmoniously with other countries to solve truly global problems. The coronavirus crisis has made the benefits of international cooperation particularly salient. Still, there are also other pressing international problems—including climate change, tax competition, and nuclear proliferation—that require serious and sustained cooperation among nations. Trade wars make such cooperation far more difficult.

The novel coronavirus has focused attention on the need to ensure that we have adequate domestic stockpiles of essential drugs and medical equipment, but the crisis does not eliminate the substantial benefits from trade.[12] On the contrary, the crisis has shown the indispensable nature of international exchange, as scientists work in globally connected groups to share insights on fighting the virus and developing a vaccine. The world is a healthier place when talented scientists throughout the world share their knowledge through collaboration and trade. In contrast, trade barriers make a bad situation worse.[13]

Immigration barriers are an even more foolish response to our economic challenges. Throughout American history, our large immigrant populations have been a source of economic strength and dynamism.[14] Immigrants bring much-needed labor market skills to our workforce, and they also create jobs, since immigrants are more entrepreneurial than their native-born counterparts. Immigrants and their children are responsible for founding over 40 percent of Fortune 500 companies, and immigrants were involved in the founding of half of our billion-dollar start-ups.[15] Because immigrants create both supply and demand for labor, there is little evidence that they have harmful effects on native-workers' employment prospects.[16]

Immigrants also fuel innovation and knowledge creation, both essential as we seek treatments and vaccines for the novel coronavirus.[17] Americans have won the majority of Nobel Prizes in scientific fields in recent decades, and a majority of these US Nobel Prizes were won by foreign-born researchers.[18] The United States is tremendously lucky to attract the world's talent to our universities and to often become the new home of many international students who decide to stay and become American citizens. We should do everything we can to retain such advantages.

Immigrants also relieve US demographic pressures.[19] The retiring of the baby-boom generation has generated heavy burdens on Social Security and Medicare programs, but the taxpayers' fiscal burdens would weigh far more heavily without the additional population growth that has resulted from recent generations of immigrants.

Unfortunately, in recent years, the US policy stance has become far less welcoming to immigrants, and our policy changes have ranged from merely wrongheaded to deeply immoral (e.g., the child separation policy).[20] Such policy steps are out of step with the best attributes of our American experience, and they also defy economic logic. These policy choices also speak to the fact that scapegoating is a more attractive policy strategy when economic growth is not widely shared. Still, the American public is less isolationist than our present policy stance might reflect. In recent years, polling data have revealed substantial majorities of people in favor of both trade and immigration.[21]

If barriers and walls are not the answer, what is? Luckily, there are many better policy solutions that go directly to the problems faced by American workers. If these strategies are pursued aggressively and wholeheartedly, we can effectively respond to those who have been left behind without sacrificing the many benefits of an open economy.

The first task is to ensure economic recovery from the coronavirus. The best public investments are in taming the virus itself, as recovery won't occur if people are fearful of going about their normal economic lives. This means investing in testing, tracing, treatment, and vaccination. But even if the virus disappeared tomorrow (which it won't), we also face the prospect of a deep recession if we don't respond with continued counter-cyclical policies. For instance, state and local governments have taken a big hit to their tax revenues, and since subnational governments are far more constrained in their borrowing, revenue shortfalls will translate into job and public service cuts, generating a large contractionary force for the whole economy.[22] In recent months, unemployment has soared to historic levels, higher than at any time since the Great Depression, and job recovery in some areas, such as travel and restaurants, is likely to be particularly slow. Continued federal spending that includes help for state governments, and continued provision of liquidity by the Federal Reserve, will be essential.

An open economy is in the interest of US workers, who benefit from the free flow of ideas, goods, services, students, entrepreneurs, and even policy solutions

Second, we need a tax system that is suited for our present economic challenges.[23] This means making sure that economic growth translates into prosperity for all and increasing the reward to work for poorer workers. This can be done by expanding the earned income tax credit, both in general and especially for childless workers; this expansion can be coupled with a higher (and indexed for inflation) minimum wage, to make sure that workers reap the benefits. The earned income tax credit is a powerful tool for making sure that our dynamic economy rewards work and creates a rising tide that lifts all boats.

Once the current crisis is over, we also need to collect more tax revenue in order to make wise investments in education, healthcare, and infrastructure, and to fund our commitments to the elderly. This can be done, at reasonable tax rates, by a combination of modest increases in rates and an expansion of the tax base to better tax capital income, monopoly rents, inheritances, and untaxed income. Also, for companies, we can better level the playing field between foreign and domestic corporate income, while raising the corporate tax rate.[24] Further, a carbon tax is long overdue; it will help seriously respond to climate change, allowing the United States the authority to work with other countries to address this important global problem.

Finally, we also need to help workers and communities that are left behind, whether due to technological progress, domestic competition, or competition from abroad.[25] Wage insurance can help workers directly, but communities also benefit from investments in infrastructure and education.

An open economy is in the interest of US workers, who benefit from the free flow of ideas, goods, services, students, entrepreneurs, and even policy solutions.[26] To retain the gains from international trade, immigration, and global capital flows, we need to modernize economic policy to suit the current era. This means serious steps to counter economic inequality, to help those left behind, and to respond aggressively to the current crisis.

Kimberly Clausing is a professor of economics at Reed College and author of Open: The Progressive Case for Free Trade, Immigration, and Global Capital.

Endnotes

1 Michael T. Owyang and Hannah G. Shell, "Measuring Trends in Income Inequality," Federal Reserve Bank of St. Louis, March 30, 2016, https://www.stlouisfed.org/publications/regional-economist/april-2016/measuring-trends-in-income-inequality; Jay Shambaugh, Ryan Nunn, Patrick Liu, and Greg Nantz, "Thirteen Facts about Wage Growth," Brookings, September 25, 2017, https://www.brookings.edu/research/thirteen-facts-about-wage-growth/.

2 Federal Reserve Economic Data, accessed June 15, 2020, https://fred.stlouisfed.org/graph/fredgraph.png?g=rcLN.

3 Max Fisher and Emma Bubola, "As Coronavirus Deepens Inequality, Inequality Worsens Its Spread," *New York Times*, March 16, 2020, https://www.nytimes.com/2020/03/15/world/europe/corona-virus-inequality.html; Kim Parker, Juliana Menasce Horowitz, and Anna Brown, "About Half of Lower-Income Americans Report Household Job or Wage Loss Due to COVID-19," Pew Research Center, April 21, 2020, https://www.pewsocialtrends.org/2020/04/21/about-half-of-lower-income-americans-report-household-job-or-wage-loss-due-to-covid-19/.

4 Jeffrey Cheng, Dave Skidmore, and David Wessel, "What's the Fed Doing in Response to the COVID-19 Crisis? What More Could It Do?," Brookings, June 12, 2020, https://www.brookings.edu/research/fed-response-to-covid19/; Sharon Parrott, Chad Stone, Chye-Ching Huang, Michael Leachman, Peggy Bailey, Aviva Aron-Dine, Stacy Dean, and Ladonna Pavetti, "CARES Act Includes Essential Measures to Respond to Public Health, Economic Crises, but More Will Be Needed," Center on Budget and Policy Priorities, March 27, 2020, https://www.cbpp.org/research/economy/cares-act-includes-essential-measures-to-respond-to-public-health-economic-crises.

5 Kimberly Clausing, "'America First' in the Time of COVID-19," *The Hill*, March 14, 2020, https://thehill.com/opinion/national-security/487571-america-first-in-the-time-of-covid-19.

6 "The China Trade Shock," accessed June 15, 2020, http://chinashock.info/.

7 Steven Brown and Pamela J. Loprest, "How Is Technological Advancement Changing the Labor Market?," Urban Institute, September 28, 2018, https://www.urban.org/urban-wire/how-technological-advancement-changing-labor-market; Jonathan B. Baker, "Market Power in the US Economy Today," Washington Center for Equitable Growth, March 20, 2017, https://equitablegrowth.org/market-power-in-the-u-s-economy-today/; US Bureau of Labor Statistics, "Union Members Summary," news release, January 22, 2020, https://www.bls.gov/news.release/union2.nr0.htm#:~:text=The%20number%20of%20wage%20and,were%2017.7%20 million%20union%20workers; Dean Baker, Josh Bivens, and Jessica Schieder, "Reining in CEO Compensation and Curbing the Rise of Inequality," Economic Policy Institute, June 4, 2019, https://www.epi.org/publication/reining-in-ceo-compensation-and-curbing-the-rise-of-inequality/; Kimberly Clausing, "Tax Policy in the New Gilded Age," *Milken Institute Review*, April 27, 2018, https://www.milkenreview.org/articles/tax-policy-in-the-new-gilded-age.

8 Jason Furman, Katheryn Russ, and Jay Shambaugh, "US Tariffs Are an Arbitrary and Regressive Tax," *VoxEU*, January 12, 2017, https://voxeu.org/article/us-tariffs-are-arbitrary-and-regressive-tax.

9 Mary Amiti, Stephen J. Redding, and David E. Weinstein, "New China Tariffs Increase Costs to US Households," *Liberty Street Economics*, Federal Reserve Bank of New York, May 23, 2019, https://libertystreeteconomics.newyorkfed.org/2019/05/new-china-tariffs-increase-costs-to-us-households.html?mod=article_inline; Jeanna Smialek and Ana Swanson, "American Consumers, Not China, Are Paying for Trump's Tariffs," *New York Times*, January 6, 2020, https://www.nytimes.com/2020/01/06/business/economy/trade-war-tariffs.html

10 . Chad P. Brown and Melina Kolb, "Trump's Trade War Timeline: An Up-to-Date Guide," *Trade and Investment Policy Watch* (blog), Peterson Institute for International Economics, March 13, 2020, https://www.piie.com/blogs/trade-investment-policy-watch/trump-trade-war-china-date-guide.

11 Sunny Glottmann, "Trump's Costly Trade Wars," Third Way, memo, February 6, 2020, https://www.thirdway.org/memo/trumps-costly-trade-wars; Ben Casselman, Niraj Chokshi, and Jim Tankersley, "The Trade War, Paused for Now, Is Still Wreaking Damage," *New York Times*, January 22, 2020, https://www.nytimes.com/2020/01/22/business/economy/trade-economy.html.

12 Kimberly A. Clausing, "Global Medical Trade in the Time of the Coronavirus Pandemic," Washington Center for Equitable Growth, May 6, 2020, https://equitablegrowth.org/global-medical-trade-in-the-time-of-the-coronavirus-pandemic/.

13 Chad P. Brown, "Trump's Trade Policy is Hampering the US Fight against COVID-19," *Trade and Investment Policy Watch* (blog), Peterson Institute for International Economics, March 13, 2020, https://www.piie.com/blogs/trade-and-investment-policy-watch/trumps-trade-policy-hampering-us-fight-against-covid-19.

14 Francine D. Blau and Christopher Mackie, eds., *The Economic and Fiscal Consequences of Immigration* (Washington, DC: National Academies Press, 2017).

15 Ian Hathaway, "Almost Half of Fortune 500 Companies Were Founded by American Immigrants or Their Children," *The Avenue* (blog), Brookings, December 4, 2017, https://www.brookings.edu/blog/the-avenue/2017/12/04/almost-half-of-fortune-500-companies-were-founded-by-american-immigrants-or-their-children/; Stuart Anderson, "Immigrants and Billion Dollar Startups" (NFAP Policy Brief, National Foundation for American Policy, Arlington, VA, March 2016), https://www.immigrationresearch.org/report/other/immigrants-and-billion-dollar-startups.

16 National Academies, *Economic and Fiscal Consequences*, 264–78.

17 Ryan Nunn, Jimmy O'Donnell, and Jay Shambaugh, "A Dozen Facts about Immigration," The Hamilton Project, Brookings, October 9, 2018, https://www.hamiltonproject.org/papers/a_dozen_facts_about_immigration.

18 Sari Pekkala Kerr, William Kerr, Çağlar Özden, and Christopher Parsons, "Global Talent Flows," *Journal of Economic Perspectives* 30, no. 4 (Fall 2016): 83–106, https://www.aeaweb.org/articles?id=10.1257/jep.30.4.83.

19 Kenneth Megan and Theresa Cardinal Brown, "America's Demographic Challenge: Understanding the Role of Immigration," Bipartisan Policy Center, August 2017, https://bipartisanpolicy.org/wp-content/uploads/2019/03/BPC-Immigration-Americas-Demographic-Challenge.pdf.

20 Sarah Pierce, "Immigration-Related Policy Changes in the First Two Years of the Trump Administration," Migration Policy Institute, May 2019, https://www.migrationpolicy.org/research/immigration-policy-changes-two-years-trump-administration.

21 "Climate Change and Russia Are Partisan Flashpoints in Public's Views of Global Threats," Pew Research Center, July 30, 2019, https://www.people-press.org/2019/07/30/climate-change-and-russia-are-partisan-flashpoints-in-publics-views-of-global-threats/; Ana Gonzalez-Barrera and Phillip Connor, "Around the World, More Say Immigrants Are a Strength Than a Burden," Pew Research Center, https://www.pewresearch.org/global/2019/03/14/around-the-world-more-say-immigrants-are-a-strength-than-a-burden/.

22 Elizabeth McNichol, Michael Leachman, and Joshuah Marshall, "States Need Significantly More Fiscal Relief to Slow the Emerging Deep Recession," Center on Budget and Policy Priorities, April 14, 2020, https://www.cbpp.org/research/state-budget-and-tax/states-need-significantly-more-fiscal-relief-to-slow-the-emerging-deep.

23 Kimberly A. Clausing, "Fixing Five Flaws of the Tax Cuts and Jobs Act" (working paper, February 3, 2020), https://papers.ssrn.com/sol3/papers.cfm?abstract_id=3397387.

24 Kimberly A. Clausing, "Options for International Tax Policy after the TCJA," Center for American Progress, January 30, 2020, https://www.americanprogress.org/issues/economy/reports/2020/01/30/479956/options-international-tax- policy-tcja/; Kimberly A. Clausing, "Taxing Multinational Companies in the 21st Century," The Hamilton Project, Brookings, January 28, 2020, https://www.hamiltonproject.org/papers/taxing_multinational_companies_in_the_21st_century.

25 Kimberly A. Clausing, "International Trade Policy That Works for US Workers," Washington Center for Equitable Growth, February 18, 2020, https://equitablegrowth.org/international-trade-policy-that-works-for-u-s-workers/.

26 Kimberly A. Clausing, *Open the Progressive Case for Free Trade, Immigration, and Global Capital* (Cambridge, MA: Harvard University Press, 2019).

CHAPTER 8

Openness Is as Important Now as It Has Ever Been

Catalina Amuedo-Dorantes

The COVID-19 pandemic has shaken the world. Faced with the lack of medical treatments and vaccines, nations around the globe have opted for the only remedy known against the easily communicable virus –namely, the adoption of social distancing measures that curtail its contagion. As the pandemic rolled from Wuhan, China, to other nations, international borders closed, quarantines were imposed on newcomers, and, overall, international mobility came to a near-complete halt.[1]

In the United States, the president's March 11 announcement of restrictions placed on international arrivals from 26 countries[2] led to the State Department's suspension of exchange programs—which allow qualified foreign-nationals to participate in work- and study-based exchange visitor programs—for at least 60 days. Participants in these exchange visitor programs include foreign-born medical school graduates who complete their residency requirements and subspecialty training in the United States prior to going back home for two years before they can return to the United States—usually through an H1-B or L-1 visa. Many of them actively helped save American lives as the pandemic spread throughout the country, either through their medical practice or through research for a COVID-19 treatment and vaccine. Yet their ability to remain in the country, and the continuation of the program itself, remain uncertain.

An important challenge in recovering from the pandemic will be fighting perceptions of immigrants as economic and security threats.

Similarly, many international students have found themselves stranded with visas that restrict their ability to work and prevent them from going back home, given their ineligibility for COVID-19-related federal assistance. On March 20, a few days after the president's announcement on travel restrictions, the US Citizenship and Immigration Services (USCIS) announced the immediate pausing of most immigrant and non-immigrant visas.[3]

On April 22, immigration restrictions were further extended when the President signed an executive order that suspended employment-based immigration, family reunification, and the diversity visa lottery program—all under the pretense of protecting American workers from the looming economic crisis. The ban, however, fit well with the stricter immigration policy climate that has characterized President Trump's administration. Soon after his inauguration in 2017, the Trump administration banned foreign nationals from eight countries from entering the United States, reduced refugee admissions, ended new applications for the Deferred Action for Childhood Arrivals (DACA) program, ended the temporary protected status (TPS) designations for Sudan, Nicaragua, Haiti, and El Salvador, and began instating "zero tolerance" policies at the border that increased child detentions and family separations.[4]

Within the first nine months of Donald Trump taking office, arrests for immigration violations increased by 42 percent, and non-border deportations rose 25 percent in 2017.[5] Overall, these actions, along with promises of significant regulatory changes to a wide range of programs, have damaged international confidence in the United States and perception of US policies abroad.[6]

An important challenge in recovering from the pandemic will be fighting perceptions of immigrants as economic and security threats. We must dispel these perceptions by creating and maintaining an open economy that welcomes the international exchange of ideas that has characterized and fueled growth in the United States for decades. If the COVID-19 pandemic has underscored anything, it is the many ways in which immigrants contribute to our economy, keeping Americans safe, healthy, and fed. Immigrants have been leading the response to the pandemic working as healthcare providers and farmworkers, in the food preparation and delivery services, as well as in cleaning and maintenance services. Families who remember the empty store shelves of March should remember the many migrant workers who continued working the land and distributing food to ensure shelves were full in April.

An important task remains the acknowledgment of migrants' contributions to our economy.

The Center for Migration Studies estimates that close to 20 million immigrants work in "essential critical infrastructure" categories.[7] One-fourth of all doctors in the United States are foreign-trained.[8] They are more likely to serve in less lucrative yet badly needed specialties, such as primary care, as well as in poorer, less educated areas with more minorities—a group that has greatly suffered during the COVID-19 pandemic.[9] Many of these doctors have been involved in research for COVID-19 treatments and a vaccine, accounting for 22 percent of all scientific researchers in the country[10] Similarly, immigrants are key in sectors ensuring Americans are well-fed. As shown in Figure 1, immigrants are vital in industries such as agriculture (26 percent), the manufacturing of food, medicine, and cleaning supplies (26 percent), essential retail and wholesale (18 percent), and transportation services (34 percent)—all sectors involved in getting food from the fields to our tables.[11]

Despite their distinct contributions to the economy and to the well-being of Americans during the pandemic, many immigrants have been largely excluded from the protections provided by Congress under the Coronavirus Aid, Relief, and Economic Security (CARES) Act and the Families First Act.[12] The CARES Act excludes not only undocumented immigrants from access to free COVID-19 testing and care but also many migrants legally residing in the United States under DACA, non-immigrant visas, tem-

Figure 1. Percentage of Foreign-Born Essential Workers

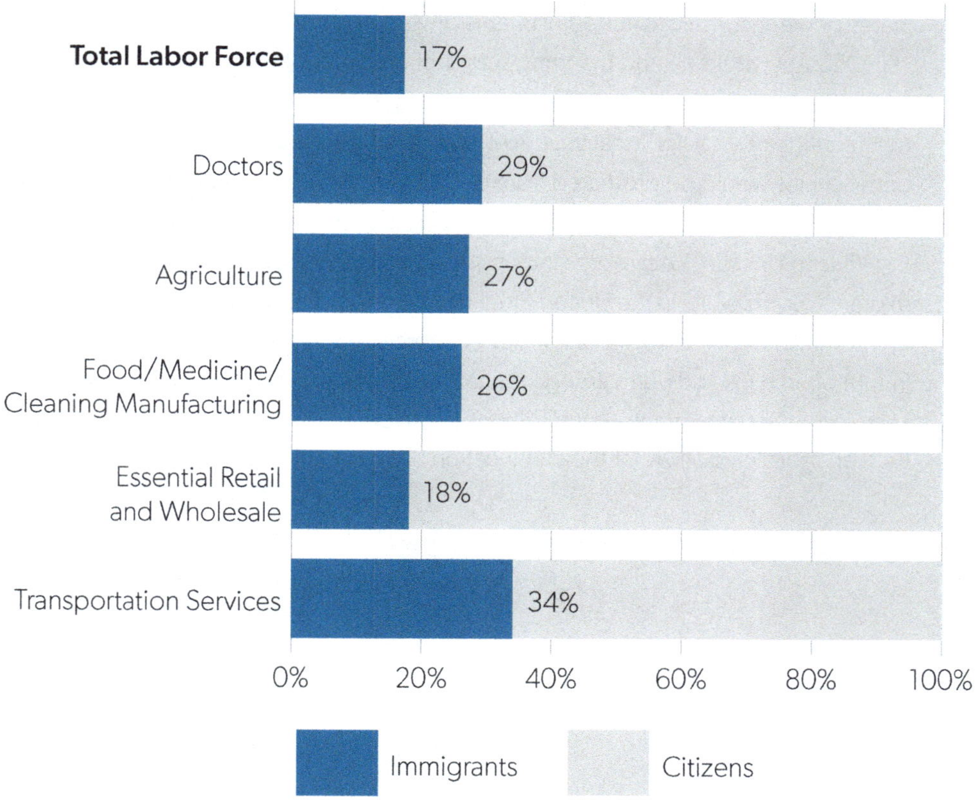

All numbers are taken from: https://www.migrationpolicy.org/sites/default/files/publications/COVID-19-EssentialWorkers-FS_Final.pdf

porary protected status, or U-visas. While some might be eligible through state-level emergency Medicaid programs, eligibility depends on whether the applicant fulfills other Medicaid eligibility requirements. Likewise, the tax rebate proposal has excluded mixed-status families and ITIN (individual taxpayer identification numbers) tax filers, obligating many of these households to continue to work, as opposed to staying safe at home during the early spread of the pandemic.

The more recent Health and Economic Recovery Omnibus Emergency Solutions (HEROES) Act, passed by Congress on May 15, 2020, is a step forward. It would bring significant relief to many immigrant families excluded from the federal assistance provided by the CARES Act. Importantly, from an immigration perspective, would be the protections provided to immigrants currently stranded due to international travel restrictions. Immigrants who were legally present in the United States at the time the

COVID-19 pandemic was declared a public health emergency would be protected from any negative consequences associated with their inability to depart the United States or meet specific status adjustments or visa extension deadlines. In addition, the HEROES Act would extend the temporary immigration status and work permits due to expire during the duration of the national emergency period, while rolling any unused non- immigrant visas for fiscal year 2020 to the following year. Finally, DACA and TPS beneficiaries would be protected from deportation for the duration their permits were initially granted, with no additional funds going to immigration enforcement.[13]

While the HEROES Act represents an important first step to reinstating and reassuring migrants' rights while in the United States, more needs to be done to ensure openness to international exchanges and a faster economic recovery. In addition to terminating immigration bans and normalizing international flows, an important task remains the acknowledgment of migrants' contributions to our economy and the adoption of policies that recognize and allow for the continuation of such valuable input.

Catalina Amuedo-Dorantes is a professor at San Diego State University.

Endnotes

1 "Coronavirus: Travel Restrictions, Border Shutdowns by Country," *Al Jazeera News*, June 3, 2020, http://www.aljazeera.com/news/2020/03/coronavirus-travel-restrictions-border-shutdowns-country-200318091505922.html; Adriaan Alsema, "With Closing of International Airports, Colombia Goes on Lockdown," *Colombia Reports*, March 19, 2020, https://colombiareports.com/with-closing-of-international-airports-colombia-goes-on-lockdown/; Centers for Disease Control and Prevention, "After You Travel," Coronavirus Disease 2019, last modified August 25, 2020, https://www.cdc.gov/coronavirus/2019-ncov/travelers/after-travel-precautions.html.

2 Donald J. Trump, Proclamation: Suspension of Entry as Immigrants and Nonimmigrants of Certain Additional Persons Who Pose a Risk of Transmitting 2019 Novel Coronavirus, March 11, 2020, https://www.whitehouse.gov/presidential-actions/proclamation-suspension-entry-immigrants-nonimmigrants-certain-additional-persons-pose-risk-transmitting-2019-novel-coronavirus/.

3 US Citizenship and Immigration Services, "USCIS Announces Temporary Suspension of Premium Processing for All I-129 and I-140 Petitions Due to the Coronavirus Pandemic," news release, last modified March 27, 2020, https://www.uscis.gov/working-united-states/temporary-workers/uscis-announces-temporary-suspension-premium-processing-all-i-129-and-i-140-petitions-due-coronavirus-pandemic.

4 Sarah Pierce and Andrew Selee, "Immigration under Trump: A Review of Policy Shifts in the Year since the Election" (Policy Brief, Migration Policy Institute, Washington, DC, December 2017).

5 "Donald Trump Takes a Hard Turn on Immigration," *The Economist*, April 5, 2018, https://www.economist.com/united-states/2018/04/05/donald-trump-takes-a-hard-turn-on-immigration.

6 These have ranged from the optional practical training (OPT) to the H1-B programs, and included attempts to adjust how the US Citizenship and Immigration Services (USCIS) calculates "unlawful presence" for international higher education students, and the recent creation of a "Denaturalization Section" by the Justice Department. Nathan Grawe, "International Students and US Higher Education," *Higher Education, EconoFact*, July 17, 2019, https://econofact.org/international-students-and-u-s-higher-education; Richard Wike, Bruce Stokes, Jacob Poushter, Laura Silver, Janell Fetterolf, and Kat Devlin, "Trump's International Ratings Remain Low, Especially among Key Allies," Pew Research Center, October 1, 2018, https://www.pewresearch.org/global/wp-content/uploads/sites/2/2018/10/Pew-Research-Center_U-S-Image-Report_UPDATED_2018-10-01.pdf.

7 Donald Kerwin, Mike Nicholson, Daniela Alulema, and Robert Warren, *US Foreign-Born Essential Workers by Status and State, and the Global Pandemic* (New York, NY: Center for Migration Studies, May 2020), https://cmsny.org/publications/us-essential-workers/.

8 American Immigration Council, *Foreign-Trained Doctors Are Critical to Serving Many US Communities*, January 17, 2018, https://www.americanimmigrationcouncil.org/research/foreign-trained-doctors-are-critical-serving-many-us-communities.

9 Rashawn Ray, "Why Are Blacks Dying at Higher Rates from COVID-19?," *FixGov* (blog), Brookings, April 9, 2020, https://www.brookings.edu/blog/fixgov/2020/04/09/why-are-blacks-dying-at-higher-rates-from-covid-19/.

10 Julia Gelatt, "Immigrant Workers: Vital to the US COVID-19 Response, Disproportionally Vulnerable," Migration Policy Institute, April 2020, https://www.migrationpolicy.org/research/immigrant-workers-us-covid-19-response.

11 American Immigration Council, "Immigrants in the United States," fact sheet, August 6, 2020, www.americanimmigrationcouncil.org/research/immigrants-in-the-united-states; Gelatt, "Immigrant Workers."

12 Migration Policy Institute, "Mixed-Status Families Ineligible for CARES Act Federal Pandemic Stimulus Check," May 2020, https://www.migrationpolicy.org/content/mixed-status-families-ineligible-pandemic-stimulus-checks.

13 Jorge Loweree, "The HEROES Act Would Provide Aid to Millions of Immigrants Left Out of Other Coronavirus Relief Packages," *Immigration Impact*, American Immigration Council, May 18, 2020, https://immigrationimpact.com/2020/05/18/heroes-act-immigrants/#.X4IWvS2ZMWo.

CHAPTER 9

Guiding Principles for Immigration Policy in a Post-Pandemic World

Michele Waslin and James Witte

The COVID-19 pandemic has shone a spotlight on inequalities in US society. By mid-November 2020, more than ten and a half million people had been diagnosed with COVID-19 and more than 243,000 people had died across all 50 states; yet not all communities have been hit evenly. Many White Americans still do not know a single person with the virus. Early data from New York City showed that the virus was killing Latinos at 1.6 times the rate of Whites.[1] In the closing weeks of June 2020, in counties where at least a quarter of the population is Latino there was a 32 percent increase in new cases, as compared to a 15 percent increase in all other counties.[2] Data from the Centers for Disease Control and Prevention in late summer 2020 shows that Hispanics and African Americans have been hit especially hard.[3] In Utah, New Jersey, Washington State, and Oregon, Latinos were approximately one and one-half to three times more likely as their population percentages to be infected.[4]

The reasons behind this disparity are many. Immigrants tend to be overrepresented in roles deemed "essential," and they continue to work in hospitals, grocery stores, restaurants, food production plants, and other locations. These roles provide them with little ability to protect themselves from close contact with others, as they provide the goods and services we all need. The foreign-born comprise 17 percent of the US workforce but 19 percent of workers in industries vital to the COVID-19 response, including 26 percent of workers in the manufacturing of food, medicine, and cleaning agents and 27 percent of workers in agriculture.[5] Immigrant workers are also disproportionate in the industries hardest hit by layoffs due to social distancing measures.[6] Noncitizens in these jobs are particularly vulnerable in that they often lack access to safety net programs such as unemployment insurance or food stamps, have lower incomes, and are less likely to have health insurance and access to healthcare.[7]

Immigrants tend to be overrepresented in roles deemed "essential," and they continue to work in hospitals, grocery stores, restaurants, and food production plants.

Despite the differential impact of COVID-19 on many immigrants, and regardless of the essential roles they have played in a struggling economy, we have seen discrimination and abuse targeting immigrants, particularly Asian Americans, and renewed calls to restrict immigration further.

Even before the pandemic, immigrant advocates saw a need to reformulate their strategies for reforming the nation's immigration system. Well-researched arguments tied to immigrant contributions to the economy and our education system were not winning the day, nor were appeals to humanitarian concerns and issues of human rights. Then the COVID-19 pandemic came and exacerbated the need for a new line of thinking. Those who support a restrictive and punitive immigration policy had new cause to go after legal and unauthorized immigrants. Double-digit unemployment and public health fears tied to a virus that has derogatorily been labeled "Chinese" have set the stage for further efforts to limit immigration. In fact, the president has already issued two proclamations restricting legal immigration under the dubious justification that it will protect American jobs.[8]

In this environment, how do academics and advocates counter anti-immigrant arguments that are short-sighted and not grounded in reasoned evidence? How do we communicate the facts regarding the critical role played by immigrants in the economy in a way that will move the public and political actors to support rational, constructive immigration policies? How do we focus on the contributions of foreign-born workers without alienating the far larger share of workers who are not foreign-born?

While the nation's response to the pandemic has been flawed—with a terrible loss of life and economic suffering—the tragedy of the pandemic and policy responses represents an opportunity for a reset in thinking to inform public deliberation. Where there has been success in response to the COVID-19 pandemic and its economic consequences, two common elements stand out: decentralized decision-making and approaches that have emphasized positive sum solutions, where benefits to an individual are not at the expense of others and may even bring benefits to others. With little clear national leadership, decisions were made at the state and local levels; calls for isolation, lockdown, and social distancing to "flatten the curve" were grounded in the argument that the health of each of us depended on the actions of all of us.

Considering the future of immigration policy, efforts to find decentralized and positive-sum solutions may be useful guiding principles to think about in the months and years to come.

Decentralized Solutions

One theme emerging from the pandemic is the value of state and local solutions. When the White House showed little leadership during the crisis, Americans turned to their governors, mayors, and state health officials, many of whom stepped in to provide their constituencies with coronavirus-related data and guidance for preventing the virus's spread.

State leadership extended benefits to immigrant communities that had been left out of federal support programs. For example, California created a $75 million cash assistance program to provide relief to unauthorized immigrants who were ineligible for federal relief programs and unemployment insurance.[9] Several other states and cities have implemented similar programs for undocumented immigrants affected by the pandemic.

The conception of states as "laboratories of democracy" that provide a testing ground for policy ideas is not new. Within the limits of federal law, for decades, states and localities have created policies intended to best deal with the daily realities of immigrants living and working within their communities. There is no national immigrant integration plan. Some states have taken the lead on integrating immigrants by providing English language instruction and naturalization assistance and by expanding eligibility for driver's licenses, healthcare, and in-state tuition for certain undocumented immigrants. In contrast, other states and localities have determined that enhanced cooperation with Immigration and Customs Enforcement (ICE) on immigration enforcement was in their best interests, though others have rejected these policies.

In the aftermath of the COVID-19 crisis, increased power sharing between the federal government, states, and localities may provide a way forward. For example, a state-based visa program that grants states a larger role in requesting the number and type of immigrant workers needed to supplement their labor force could be on the table.[10] Given the unevenness of the economic downturn and recovery following the pandemic, states may welcome a nimbler immigration system that is responsive to their unique economies and labor needs. Other states may choose not to participate due to a combination of high unemployment rates and anti-immigrant sentiment.

However, it is not at all clear that even the reddest of states are eager to reject legal immigration. In September 2019, President Trump issued an executive order requiring states to consent, in writing, to resettle refugees. This came with the assumption that, given the choice, states would choose to reject refugees. In fact, the governors of 42 states consented, and only Texas refused before a federal judge blocked the executive order. While not required to do so, more than 100 mayors also sent the White House letters welcoming refugees to their cities.[11]

If the United States is to move further down the immigration federalism path, the federal government must provide leadership. History has shown that the "laboratories of democracy" have their limits, and clear lines must be drawn to ensure that acting in their own self-interest does not result in discrimination, abuse, and civil rights violations. Just as early, strong federal leadership could have slowed the spread of the virus and decreased confusion over proper safety measures and reopening the economy, Congress, the courts, and the White House have a role to play in setting the parameters within which states may act.

Positive-Sum Solutions

Thomas Friedman's critically acclaimed book, *The World Is Flat: A Brief History of the Twenty-First Century*, was widely seen as a harbinger of a new world order. In a "flattened" world, people are interconnected on a level playing field in which all competitors have equal opportunity. Within the new economic and social order, the strongest, fastest, and smartest succeed.[12] A motif of competition runs throughout the book. For example, Friedman explains that "every morning in Africa, a gazelle wakes up. It knows it must run faster than the fastest lion, or it will be killed. Every morning a lion wakes up. It knows it must outrun the slowest gazelle, or it will starve to death. It doesn't matter whether you are a lion or a gazelle. When the sun comes up, you better start running."

Taken at face value, protectionist trade policies and restrictive immigration policies appear to align with Friedman's arguments about competition. If you want to stay ahead of the other gazelles, then you may support policies that slow them down; as a ravenous lion, you may seek to quickly breach any natural or human-made barriers that protect the gazelles as they graze.

However, Friedman's story is as much about collaboration as it is about competition, as can be seen in his rules for how businesses can best cope in a flat world.

> Rule #1: "When the world goes flat—and you are feeling flattened—reach for a shovel and dig inside yourself. Don't try to build walls."

In the short run, a hardening of borders—on international travel and trade, and also within the United States—may be necessary to slow the spread of the coronavirus. In the long run, however, maintaining such restrictions, including constructing a "big, beautiful wall," undermines the collaboration essential to mutual prosperity:

> Rule #4: "The best companies are the best collaborators. In the flat world, more and more business will be done through collaborations within and between companies, for a very simple reason: The next layers of value creation—whether in technology, marketing, biomedicine, or manufacturing—are becoming so complex that no single firm or department is going to be able to master them alone."

This second part of Friedman's story cautions us against viewing the world as a zero-sum game, where every gain that one individual or one group makes comes at the cost of another individual or another group. In contrast, a key insight from economics that informs Friedman's writing is that many interactions are positive-sum. They grow the pie and allow for bigger slices for all.

Zero-sum thinking is the basis of the "immigrants are taking our jobs" argument. The arguments are questionable as anti-immigrant groups were making this claim when the US national unemployment rate was under 4 percent. These claims have grown even louder as we enter a sustained period of double-digit unemployment. But these arguments remain suspect as they fail to recognize how immigrants also grow job opportunities for everyone.[13] According to labor economist Mark Regets, policy like the president's immigration restrictions "... assumes there is a fixed number of jobs, which no economist believes, that any new entrant into the labor market must take a job from someone else, and cites a number about lost jobs without noting that research shows hiring people in high-skilled positions often supports jobs for other workers at a company."[14] The labor force is a pie that can grow; with more open immigration policies and wider recognition that immigrants help to grow the pie, the labor market can be a positive-sum solution.

A positive-sum approach would emphasize the added value that immigrant workers bring to the nation's response to COVID-19 and to rebuilding the economy. Not only are foreign-born workers "essential" during the pandemic, but they will also be critical to rebuilding the post-pandemic economy. Native-born US workers will always be the majority of workers in most industries in most areas of the country. The foreign-born labor force provides an important complement to the native workforce—in specific industries and in particular geographic areas, but also in the economy at large. Recent US census data show that the non-working age population (age 0 to 14 and 65 and older) is growing faster than the working-age population. Between 2010 and 2019, the non-working-age population grew by 13.1 million, while the working-age population increased by only 6.4 million.[15] Foreign-born workers help to balance that trend. The foreign-born labor force is disproportionately younger than native-born workers and is literally doing more of the heavy lifting. For example, in Northern Virginia, 56.5 percent of Latino workers living in households with total incomes of less than 150 percent of the poverty line are concentrated in three essential occupational groups—food preparation and service, buildings and grounds cleaning and maintenance, and construction—as contrasted to just 20.5 percent of non-Latino workers in similar households. Moreover, in the latter two groups, the average age of Latino workers is approximately four years younger than non-Latinos.

A positive-sum approach would emphasize the added value that immigrant workers bring to the nation's response to COVID-19 and to rebuilding the economy.

A further example of a mutually beneficial positive-sum approach can be seen in the connections between public health, immigration, and vaccination clearly evident in the COVID-19 pandemic. We can only contain the virus if all individuals, regardless of immigration status, have access to testing, healthcare, and, eventually, vaccination. Vaccines can facilitate herd immunity, when approximately 70 percent of a population has acquired immunity either through a vaccine or naturally through recovery from COVID-19.[16] However, if a significant number of individuals—including immigrants whose immigration status leaves them vulnerable—do not receive a vaccination, then the risk of infection and disease goes up dramatically for everyone in the population. While the spread of communicable disease is a global phenomenon, initial outbreaks are local. Estimates suggest that there are 10.7 million undocumented immigrants in the United States. Nationwide the undocumented population accounts for just over 3 percent of the population; however, the undocumented population is locally concentrated, not evenly distributed. For example, in Las Vegas, over 8 percent of the metro population is estimated to be unauthorized.[17] If immigration status reduces vaccine adoption, then the health of the entire country is compromised as local outbreaks have been difficult to contain.

Forging a Way Forward

The efficacy of decentralized policymaking and positive-sum solutions are not unrelated but rather complement one another. Decentralized decision-making sets the stage for a sense of common identity and the pursuit of mutually beneficial, positive-sum solutions adapted to local context. At the state and local levels, stakeholders are most likely to identify and endorse choices that bring people together around common interests. Decentralized decision-making may lead to additional California-like solutions that prioritize the public health of all over punishing unauthorized immigrants for their inability to work legally in the United States. States already can ease licensing requirements so that foreign-born workers can obtain the documentation needed to work. Taken even further, if state leaders have more authority over immigration policy, they are in a better position to ensure that adequate numbers of foreign healthcare workers will be able to work in their states.

Successfully pursuing such strategies around immigration policy in the face of COVID-19 may establish a framework for addressing multiple other policy issues that have received woefully inadequate responses. Climate change, immigration reform, economic inequality, and an aging transportation and utility infrastructure are examples of national and global problems that have long been recognized but where responses have been piecemeal and insular at best. COVID-19 is a public health risk that we cannot kick down the road. Recognizing that immigrants are part of the solution—both in terms of public health and economic recovery—and developing appropriate decentralized policy responses advancing our common interests may offer lessons for a path forward in other policy domains.

Michele Waslin is the program coordinator at the Institute for Immigration Research at George Mason University.

James Witte is a professor in the Department of Sociology and Anthropology at George Mason University, the director of the Center for Social Science Research, and the director of the Institute for Immigration Research.

Endnotes

1 NYC Health, "Age-Adjusted Rates of Lab Confirmed COVID-19 Non-hospitalized Cases, Estimated Non-fatal Hospitalized Cases, and Patients Known to Have Died 100,000 by Race/Ethnicity Group as of April 16, 2020," City of New York, April 16, 2020, https://www1.nyc.gov/assets/doh/downloads/pdf/imm/covid-19-deaths-race-ethnicity-04162020-1.pdf, accessed November 13, 2020.

2 Julia Gelatt, "Immigrant Workers: Vital to the US COVID-19 Response, Disproportionately Vulnerable," Migration Policy Institute, March 2020, https://www.migrationpolicy.org/research/immigrant-workers-us-covid-19-response.

3 Centers for Disease Control and Prevention, "COVID-19 Hospitalization and Death by Race/Ethnicity," https://www.cdc.gov/coronavirus/2019-ncov/covid-data/investigations-discovery/hospitalization-death-by-race-ethnicity.html.Accessed , accessed November 13, 2020.

4 NJ Health, "New Jersey Statistics: COVID Confirmed Case Summary," New Jersey Department of Health, https://www.nj.gov/health/cd/documents/topics/NCOV/COVID_Confirmed_Case_Summary.pdf accessed November 10, 2020; Nancy Bood, Ariel Ferguson, Kyle Kaupp, Amanda Mathis, and Rick Igou, "Oregon COVID-19 Daily Update," State of Oregon, https://govsite-assets.s3.amazonaws.com/UOuDmQc5Rf2TVQG4k4r0_Oregon-COVID-19-Update-04-16-2020-FINAL.pdf, accessed November 10, 2020; Utah Department of Health, "Overview," COVID-19 Surveillance, 2020, https://coronavirus.utah.gov/case-counts/, accessed November 10, 2020; Washington State Department of Health, "2019 Novel Coronavirus Outbreak (COVID-19)," https://www.doh.wa.gov/emergencies/coronavirus, accessed November 10, 2020.

5 Julia Gelatt, "Immigrant Workers."

6 Ibid.

7 Ibid.

8 Stuart Anderson, "New Trump H-1B Visa Restrictions Will Harm Companies," *Forbes*, June 23, 2020, https://www.forbes.com/sites/stuartanderson/2020/06/23/new-trump-h-1b-visa-restrictions-will-harm-companies/#1ef3999770e8.

9 Miriam Jordan, "California Offers $500 in Covid-19 Aid to Undocumented Immigrants," *New York Times*, May 18, 2020, https://www.nytimes.com/2020/05/18/us/coronavirus-undocumented-california.html.

10 Michele Waslin, *Immigration at the State Level: An Examination of Proposed State-Based Visa Programs in the US* (Washington, DC: Bipartisan Policy Center, May 2020), https://bipartisanpolicy.org/download/?file=/wp-content/uploads/2020/05/BPC_Immigration_State-Based-Visa-Programs-Final4.pdf; Adam Ozimek, Kenan Fikri, and John Lettieri, *From Managing Decline to Building the Future: Could a Heartland Visa Help Struggling Regions?* (Washington, DC: Economic Innovation Group, April 2019), https://eig.org/wp-content/uploads/2019/04/Heartland-Visas-Report.pdf.

11 Lutheran Immigration and Refugee Services, "Latest Developments on Refugee Resettlement Consent," LIRS, January 2, 2020, https://www.lirs.org/refugee-consents-2020.

12 Thomas Friedman, *The World is Flat: A Brief History of the Twenty-First Century* (New York: Macmillan, 2005).

13 Shai Bernstein, Rebecca Diamond, Timothy McQuade, and Beatriz Pousada, "The Contributions of High-Skilled Immigrants to Innovation in the United States" (Stanford Graduate School of Business Working Paper No. 3748, Stanford University, Stanford, CA, November 6, 2018), https://www.gsb.stanford.edu/faculty-research/working-papers/contribution-high-skilled-immigrants-innovation-united-states; Giovanni Peri, Kevin Shih, and Chad Sparber, "STEM Workers, H-1B Visas, and Productivity in US Cities" *Journal of Labor Economics* 33, no. 3 (July 2015): S225-S255; Nicole Kreisberg, "H-1B Visas: No Impact on Wages," American Institute for Economic Research, issue brief, October 9, 2014, https://www.aier.org/research/h-1b-visas-no-impact-on-wages/; Giovanni Peri, Kevin Shih, and Chad Sparber., *Closing Economic Windows: How H-1B Visa Denials Cost US-Born Tech Workers Jobs and Wages During the Great Recession* (New York: Partnership for a New American Economy, June 2014), http://www.renewoureconomy.org/wp-content/uploads/2014/06/pnae_h1b.pdf; Madeline Zavodny, "The H-1B

Program and Its Effects on Information Technology Workers," *Federal Reserve Bank of Atlanta Economic Review* 88, no. 3 (September 2003): 33–43, https://www.frbatlanta.org/research/publications/economic-review/2003/q3/vol88no3_H-1B-program-and-effects-on-information-technology-workers.

14 Stuart Anderson, "New Trump H-1B Visa Restrictions Will Harm Companies," *Forbes*, June 23, 2020, https://www.forbes.com/sites/ stuartanderson/2020/06/23/new-trump-h-1b-visa-restrictions-will-harm- companies/#1214aacc70e8.

15 Luke Rogers and Kristie Wilder, "Working-Age Population Not Keeping Pace with Growth in Older Americans," US Census Bureau, June 25, 2020, https://www.census.gov/library/stories/2020/06/working-age-population-not-keeping-pace-with-growth-in-older-americans.html.

16 Kin On Kwok, Florence Lai, Samuel Yeung Shan Wong, and Julian W. T. Tang, "Herd Immunity: Estimating the Level Required to Halt the COVID-19 Epidemics in Affected Countries," *Journal of Infection* 80, no. 6 (March 2020): e32–e33, https://www.journalofinfection.com/article/S0163-4453(20)30154-7/fulltext.

17 Jeffrey S. Passel and D'Vera Cohn, "20 Metro Areas Are Home to Six-in-Ten Unauthorized Immigrants in US," *Fact Tank*, Pew Research Center, March 11, 2019, https://www.pewresearch.org/fact-tank/2019/03/11/us-metro-areas-unauthorized-immigrants.

CHAPTER 10

A Proposal for Immigration Reform

Alan M. Kraut

Introduction

The COVID-19 crisis threatens to disrupt patterns of migration crucial to global economic recovery. As an American immigration historian and a nonresident fellow of the Migration Policy Institute, I offer a path to turn the current conversation away from the threat of greater immigration restriction toward a more constructive discussion of policy reform.

The COVID-19 public health crisis has stunningly reminded Americans of a critical characteristic of the country's workforce: the contributions of the foreign-born who have emigrated to the United States. Data compiled by the Migration Policy Institute, a Washington, DC-based think-tank, indicates that immigrants account for 18 percent, or 2.6 million, of the estimated 14.7 million people employed in healthcare in the United States.[1] They are concentrated in certain key occupations. Twenty-eight percent of all US physicians are foreign-born, as are 24 percent of dentists, 38 percent of home health aides, and 26 percent of personal care aides. Such data suggest the critical need for immigration policy reform that would allow healthcare to be enriched by the skills and energy of immigrants and refugees to this country. However, the healthcare industry is only the most immediate of concerns.

In addition to their role fighting the pandemic, newcomers, whatever their immigration status, are likely to play a critical role in reconstructing a United States now in economic shambles. Recall that following the devastation of New Orleans by Hurricane Katrina, foreign-born construction workers, legal and unauthorized, rebuilt the city. The low cost of agricultural produce has also long depended upon a migrant labor force from south of our borders and again of varied legal status.

At the other end of the economy, foreign-born technological innovators and entrepreneurs have long stimulated our economy with their insights and investments. The United States issues more patents—evidence of innovation—than any country in the world, and immigrants have received about a quarter of them in the past decade. At Intel, the world's largest maker of semiconductors, 40 percent of the patents are for innovations developed by Chinese or East Indian immigrants. Immigrants create patents at twice the rate of native-born Americans because they disproportionately earn degrees in science and engineering as well as other STEM fields. They comprise 24 percent of the US science and engineering workforce holding bachelor's degrees and 47 percent of science and engineering workers who have PhDs. Some return to their home countries, but many continue their relationship with the American economy by staying here or communicating long-distance via the Internet. Immigrants have started 52 percent of Silicon Valley's technology companies, co-founding firms such as Google, Intel, eBay, and Yahoo.[2]

A recent presidential executive order suspended for 60 days the issuance of green cards, although there were exemptions for medical workers and some others deemed vital in the current crisis. Immigrant advocates fear that such restrictions will proliferate and become part of a new restrictionism. However, aside from zealously securing the border with walls of concrete and paper walls of regulations, there has been no real discussion about how to craft an admissions policy that meets the economic needs of the United States and would position this country to participate in a global economic recovery.[3]

What might such a plan look like?

Admission Priorities

The cornerstone of revised legal immigration policy must be occupational preference. The concept of occupational preference is hardly new. Previous legislation passed by Congress, such as the 1965 Hart-Celler Act and the 1986 Immigration Reform and Control Act, included occupational preference provisions. Less clear has been the extent to which occupational preference should outweigh other categories of admissions preference such as family reunification and how that preference system should be determined in a way that allows for a robust but flexible policy that is responsive to changes in the economy, especially technological and scientific innovations. It is also imperative that prioritizing the admission of those in needed occupations is not then undermined by denying those engaged in such necessary occupations ample opportunity for employment after arrival.[4]

The needs of reconstructing the American economy demand that occupational preference be made the highest priority in any reform of immigration policy for both white-collar and blue-collar jobs. Implementation and planning are key. In the past, point systems have been used to give preference to those in some occupations over others. Some reformers have favored lottery systems as fairer. However, more recently, some scholars pondering US immigration reform have suggested that instead of the randomness of lotteries, or a point system that must be updated regularly to reflect changes in labor market needs, that there be a system of employer-based auctions such as those in Australia, whereby employers choose the workers that they view as most likely to contribute to their profitability.[5] Seasonal labor needs will also require a temporary work visa program that is more robust and better regulated than the current system, to protect temporary workers from exploitation and unsafe labor conditions.

More important than which system of selection is implemented is that it reflects a commitment to economic pragmatism and that the mechanism for determining which occupational categories are preferred be determined in such a way that immigration policy is less of a political football than it has been in the past.

Implementation and Planning – The Machinery of Change

In recent years, immigration has been an issue of intense partisan polarization. In another era of partisan polarization, the turn of the 20th century, Progressive reformers—Democrats and Republicans— turned to non-partisan structures—commissions—to ameliorate, although not eliminate bloody political battles. This is an idea worth revisiting, though, by creating an Immigration Admissions Commission.[6]

The Immigration Admissions Commission would need to include representation of labor, manufacturing, agriculture, and new technologies as well as bipartisan participation. It would not be an advisory board but an independent body with binding regulatory authority, much like the US Security and Exchange Commission or the Board of Governors of the Federal Reserve System. The latter is appointed by the president and confirmed by the Senate for staggered 14-year terms. This commission would be the organizational structure to create five-year plans to determine how immigration admissions (number and occupational preference) might be adjusted for the subsequent five years to serve the economy's needs best. The fact that the plan could be altered every five years in response to data-driven studies might curb (though unlikely eliminate entirely) the virulent partisanship that currently diminishes the possibility of reform. Long-term appointments to the commission would enhance the likelihood of members forming relationships that would encourage compromise and an atmosphere of comity among commissioners representing different interests.

> ***There must be an extensive expansion of enforcement, including a process of application adjudication that is fair and compassionate, regardless of the cost.***

In addition to its deliberations on five-year plans for legal immigration admission, a subcommittee of this Immigration Admission Commission would also make recommendations for regulating issuance of temporary visitor work visas and altruistic admissions based upon humanitarian concerns, including family reunification. Current definitions of "refugee" and "asylee" would be retained, and the number of individuals in these categories would be adjusted annually by the commission in response to humanitarian concerns.

Immigrant Policy

Since the late 19th century, the United States government has created policies that govern the number of people who are admitted into the country and the criteria for admission. However, we do little on the federal level to aid the incorporation of immigrants into society, especially the economy. The federal government neither conducts nor subsidizes language training or job training for immigrants, nor does it provide job placement services, continuing education, or protection against workplace exploitation. That obligation is left to private agencies and state and local governments, placing an undue hardship on poorer states and localities. This must change. Moreover, these same opportunities should be extended to workers born in the United States. No policy will succeed if it seems to give an unfair advantage to immigrants at the expense of the native-born. Moreover, such additional opportunities will enhance the ability of American workers to compete on an even plane with immigrant arrivals, though there is little evidence that immigrants threaten the jobs of American workers. Overall, the American educational system needs to focus more on vocational training and an apprenticeship program like that in Germany, which would benefit natives and newcomers alike.

Immigration reform should expand immigration, not contract it. Immigration is advantageous to America's economic growth and to our role in a global recovery.

Newcomers, as well as natives, would benefit enormously from an educational reorientation that would offer young women and men marketable skills, especially those important to revitalizing our infrastructure. Many opinion writers have spoken of the need for a national service corps designed on the New Deal model of the Civilian Conservation Corps or the Works Progress Administration.[7] Job training could begin in this new national service and continue in vocational training and apprenticeship programs.

Unauthorized Immigration and a Path to Legalization

A major stumbling block to agreement on immigration reform has been the fate of unauthorized immigrants. Over the past decade, estimates of how many unauthorized are in the population vary from nine to over eleven million. Among Washington policymakers, the word "amnesty" has become a forbidden utterance. However, the last full amnesty was issued by President Ronald Reagan as part of the agreement over the 1986 Immigration and Reform Act (IRCA). The current debate is most contentious over what penalty ought to be exacted from those who have come unauthorized. Some demand fines; others insist upon deportation and application for admission after 10 years. The controversy over the Deferred Action for Childhood Arrivals (DACA) program has led some unauthorized immigrants to despair. They feel that they may never be the recipients of any compassion or leniency.[8] Many proposals work to distance newcomers from society rather than promote integration with the communities where they reside.

An alternative proposal might be a community service program administered under state and local supervision. Unauthorized immigration breaks American law. However, American law is not all of a kind. Some violations of immigration law, such as entering the United States in an unauthorized fashion, constitute a violation of administrative law only (punishable by exclusion or deportation) but do not constitute a felony under criminal law. However, certain violations of immigration law may also be violations of criminal law, and certain criminal behavior can result in immigration penalties. An example of the former includes illegal reentry, fraud, or smuggling, while examples of the latter include certain federal or state crimes that subject the individual to imprisonment and then deportation.[9] An individual violating immigration law but not criminal law may be detained pending removal proceedings to be certain that they will appear for their hearing, but the detainment is not a criminal punishment. Just as some Americans who break criminal laws are assigned community service, the government might institute a system of assigning community service to unauthorized immigrants who have broken only administrative law. Such community service supervised by state or local authorities would allow some unauthorized newcomers who have broken administrative law to remain in the United States while strengthening relationships with their neighbors and communities. For example, those who earn their livings in construction or lawn services could dedicate their service assignment to repairing or restoring local parks and playgrounds. Those with childcare skills could put those to use at community institutions such as childcare services. The community service would have a finite time limit (e.g., two years) and be regulated so as not to interfere with the occupational and family obligations of newcomers.

The United States issues more patents—evidence of innovation—than any country in the world, and immigrants have received about a quarter of them in the past decade.

Border Enforcement

Every sovereign nation has an obligation to control its borders for the benefit of its citizens and to do so in a spirit of compassion and generosity toward those who wish to enter. It is unlikely that in the foreseeable future there will be a cessation of unauthorized efforts by migrants to enter the United States. Walls, checkpoints, and interdictions by US Border Patrol will not disappear. There must be an extensive expansion of enforcement, including a process of application adjudication that is fair and compassionate, regardless of the cost. The reality of children separated from their parents at our borders contradicts the basic human values that we as a nation have historically professed. It must cease.

Electronic capabilities such as E-Verify, used to check the legal status of job applicants, must be encouraged and expanded. While individual identity cards for all residents of the United States often receive negative responses, other forms of identification using biomarkers are possibilities to be explored to identify newcomers who have overstayed visas.

Conclusion

Immigration reform should expand immigration, not contract it. Immigration is advantageous to America's economic growth and to our role in a global recovery. However, this expansion will require greater planning and preparation for integrating immigration into a long-term economic comeback. Throughout its history, the United States has tapped into a reservoir of talent and energy from other societies and cultures to great success. From the earliest days of our country, immigration has been a source of talent and energy. Now it must be regulated so that the flow of talent is consciously directed at growing the economy while helping newcomers fulfill their desire for opportunity.

Alan M. Kraut is Distinguished Professor of History at American University and a nonresident fellow of the Migration Policy Institute.

Endnotes

1 Jeanne Batalova, "Immigrant Health-Care Workers in the United States," Migration Policy Institute, May 14, 2020, https://www.migrationpolicy.org/article/immigrant-health-care-workers-united-states-2018.

2 Angelos Angelou, "How Foreign-Born Workers Spark Employment and Innovation," Xconomy, November 12, 2014, https://xconomy.com/texas/2015/11/12/how-foreign-born-workers-spark-employment-and-innovation/.

3 Ming Hsu Chen and Zachary New, "Silence and the Second Wall," *Southern California Interdisciplinary Law Journal* 28, no. 3 (Spring 2019): 549–88; Carolyn J. Heinrich, "Presidential Address: 'A Thousand Petty Fortresses': Administrative Burden in US Immigration Policies and Its Consequences," *Journal of Policy Analysis and Management* 37, no. 2 (January 2018): 211–39.

4 Other countries, such as Australia, have sometimes erred in creating additional hurdles to employment after admission for those who were given occupational preference because they were regarded as potentially benefiting the Australian economy. See Massimillano Tani, "Selective Immigration, Occupational Licensing, and Labour Market Outcomes of Foreign-Trained Migrants" (IZA Discussion Paper No. 11370, IZA Institute of Labor Economics, Bonn, Germany, February 2018).

5 Pia Orrenius and Madeline Zavodny, "An Auctions Approach to Immigration Policy" (IZA Policy Paper No. 151, IZA Institute of Labor Economics, Bonn, Germany, February 2020), http://ftp.iza.org/pp151.pdf.

6 A.C. Pigou, *The Economics of Welfare*, 4th ed. (New York: Macmillan, 1932), 332–33. Pigou, among others, has reservations about such commissions because of the possibility that they will merely become the engines to serve the interests of organizations or individuals represented on such bodies.

7 David Brooks, "We Need National Service. Now," *New York Times*, May 7, 2020, https://www.nytimes.com/2020/05/07/opinion/national-service-americorps-coronavirus.html.

8 Michelangelo Landgrave, "Scrap DACA in Favor of Long-term Reform," *Medium*, May 14, 2020, https://medium.com/cgo-benchmark/scrap-daca-in-favor-of-long-term-reform- b2e2684a87a8.

9 Immigration law enforcement requires what some scholars have characterized as the "complex interplay" of criminal and administrative law. See Cristobal Ramón and Theresa Cardinal Brown, "Decriminalizing Illegal Border Crossing: What Does It Mean? An Explainer of Civil vs. Criminal Immigration Enforcement," video blog, Bipartisan Policy Center, January 15, 2020, https://bipartisanpolicy.org/blog/decriminalizing-illegal-border-crossing-what-does-it-mean-an-explainer-of-civil-vs-criminal-immigration-enforcement/.

CHAPTER 11

Lessons on Immigration during COVID-19

Neeraj Kaushal

In the middle of the COVID-19 pandemic and national lockdowns, many Western governments sought out foreign workers to do essential jobs. In May of 2020, Italy granted a temporary six-month amnesty to 600,000 undocumented workers to ameliorate shortages of seasonal agriculture workers. Germany airlifted 40,000 foreign farmworkers in April and another 40,000 in May from Romania, Bulgaria, Hungary, and Ukraine to pick fruits and vegetables. Additionally, the German government raised seasonal farmworkers' length of stay from 70 days to 115 days.

Normally, foreign doctors in Germany must prove their credentials by passing medical licensing exams to work as physicians. During the pandemic, this licensing requirement has been waived. Even the regional medical board of Saxony, the center of the nationalist and anti-immigration party Alternative for Germany, has welcomed foreign doctors without a German license, including Syrian refugees, to treat COVID-19 patients.

Recent measures to limit the entry of foreign workers create obstacles in the path of economic recovery. The United States should increase, not decrease, avenues for legal entry into the country.

Farm owners in the United Kingdom have also started chartered flights to bring workers from Poland and Romania to pick fruit. Yes, the same Romanian and Polish workers that Brexit has pledged to ban from entry into the UK.[1] It turns out that 98 percent of vegetable and fruit pickers in the UK are foreigners, making it hard to do without them. Without these foreigners, fruits and vegetables would rot in the fields.

In the United States, while President Trump has imposed restrictions on several visa categories, the US Citizen and Immigration Services (USCIS) is making sure that essential foreign workers are allowed to enter the country. It relaxed the conditions of H-2A visas for legal seasonal agriculture workers and allowed them to stay longer than the three-year maximum allowable period. All employers with valid temporary labor certifications are allowed to hire foreign workers who are currently in the United States on H-2A visas.

In New York, the epicenter of COVID-19 in the United States in the initial months of the outbreak, Governor Andrew Cuomo issued an executive order to allow "graduates of foreign medical schools having at least one year of graduate medical education to provide patient care in hospitals" even if they do not have licenses. Abroad, the US consulates continue to process visa applications for health workers, even though the state department has closed consulate offices globally to protect the staff from the contagion.

These examples highlight the key roles immigrants play in western countries and provide several important lessons for policy.

One: Immigrants are indispensable for critical industries. The US Department of Homeland Security defines certain jobs in health, infrastructure, manufacturing, services, and food industry services as essential critical infrastructure jobs. Estimates by the Center for Migration Studies show that 69 percent of all immigrants in the labor force and 74 percent of all undocumented workers work in these essential critical infrastructure jobs.[2] As the economy recovers from COVID-19 and the resulting lockdowns, any design to impose additional restrictions on immigration would restrict the supply of workers in these essential industries and delay recovery. Recent measures by President Trump to limit the entry of foreign workers within several non-immigrant categories will create obstacles in the path of economic recovery. The United States should increase, not decrease, avenues for legal entry into the country.

Two: Policy analysts need to rethink the contributions of immigrants engaged in low-skilled occupations. The conventional wisdom is that highly skilled immigrants, including scientists, physicians, engineers, and entrepreneurs, bring enormous benefits to the host country, whereas low-skilled immigrants are a fiscal burden, and their entry should be restricted if not banned. This is the basis of merit-based and points-based immigration systems that some countries, including Canada and Australia, have adopted. There is an active debate about introducing such a system in the United States. Temporary shifts in immigration policies in a number of Western countries during COVID-19 show that this conventional wisdom has no basis. It has become clear during the lockdowns that low-skilled and even illegal immigrants play a crucial role in host countries. Their contribution should be acknowledged. Governments should integrate, not alienate, immigrants.

Yet most immigrants, in particular the undocumented, were not eligible for the provisions of the various COVID-19-linked stimulus programs in the United States, including the Coronavirus Aid, Relief, and Economic Security (CARES) Act. "Immigrants in our communities are having to make a choice between feeding their children and sending money to feed families back home," said Jairo Guzman, executive director of Mexican Coalition, a New York-based NGO, in a conversation over the phone. Mexican Coalition surveyed 160 Mexicans in New York City when the lockdowns began. Two-thirds of the respondents said that they did not have the money to purchase the basic necessities for themselves or their families for a period of just 14 days. Many said they barely had the income to purchase seven days of food and other household items.

Immigrants played a vital part and continue to work in essential industries during the COVID-19 pandemic. Alas, the federal government let them down by excluding many groups of immigrants from the CARES Act. State governments and civil rights organizations filled the gap.[3] Given the current political climate in Washington, advocacy groups are likely to achieve more success in pushing state and local governments for programs and policies to relieve immigrants of economic and health challenges inflicted by COVID-19 and the lockdown.

Three: An important lesson from the current pandemic is that immigrant health and lives matter. This is true for their own sake as well as for the sake of native-born citizens. Yet the changes to the public charge rule in February 2020 endangered both immigrants and natives by discouraging immigrants from seeking medical advice and care.[4] Given the current political climate, local and state governments need to step up to provide for the healthcare needs of immigrants who are excluded. Local and state governments need to take a more expansive and humanitarian view of healthcare to protect both the lives and livelihoods of immigrants.

Despite the value and importance of immigrant workers, COVID-19 threatens to feed nationalistic and anti-immigrant forces within Western societies. In the United States, President Trump's recent measures to restrict visas have brought many existing channels of immigration that propel vibrancy into the US labor market to a halt. These measures do not protect American workers; instead, they threaten to cripple essential sectors that are highly dependent on immigration and will set back the recovery.

State governments, advocacy groups, corporate America, and civil rights organizations should challenge these measures in order to rebuild America from the ashes of COVID-19. The pandemic brought lockdowns that sapped America's economic and social vitality. Infusing and integrating immigrants can restore this vitality. It is the only path to make America great again.

Neeraj Kaushal is a professor of social policy at Columbia University and a research associate at the National Bureau of Economic Research.

Endnotes

1 Neeraj Kaushal, *Blaming Immigrants: Nationalism and the Economics of Global Movement* (New York, NY: Columbia University Press, 2019).

2 Donald Kerwin, Mike Nicholson, Daniela Alulema, and Robert Warren, *US Foreign-Born Essential Workers by Status and State, and the Global Pandemic* (New York, NY: Center for Migration Studies, May 2020), https://cmsny.org/publications/us-essential-workers/.

3 Whitney L. Duncan and Sarah B. Horton, "Serious Challenges and Potential Solutions for Immigrant Health during COVID-19," *Health Affairs Blog*, April 18, 2020, https://www.healthaffairs.org/do/10.1377/hblog20200416.887086/full.

4 Kathleen R. Page, Maya Venkataramani, Chris Beyrer, and Sarah Polk, "Undocumented US Immigrants and COVID-19," *New England Journal of Medicine* 382, no. 21 (May 2020), https://www.nejm.org/doi/full/10.1056/NEJMp2005953.

CHAPTER 12

The Ethics of Immigration and Economic Recovery

Bas van der Vossen

COVID-19 has changed our world. One of the ways it has is by massively reducing international mobility. We travel much less for business and pleasure, of course. But international migration has been limited significantly as well. To name but one example, early in the crisis, the Trump administration banned issuing new green cards for most immigrants.

The green card ban was initially imposed for 60 days, in line with the cited justification of stopping the spread of the virus from one country to another. But the president has expressed the desire for the measure (or something approximating it) to become permanent.

Can such more permanent measures be justified in a world containing viruses like COVID-19? At some point, this virus will cease to be the threat it is today. But other viruses like it may appear in the future. So, what's to be done? Looking toward post-crisis economic and social recovery, the question of immigration will become increasingly important again.

The point of this piece is to address this question's justification. That is, it will address whether, from an economic and an ethical point of view, the restrictions on immigration that exist today can be defensibly continued once the current threat of COVID-19 has been brought under control. It may be tempting today to accept a kind of reasoning of "as in crisis, so in normal times." The question is whether that is acceptable.

Let us begin with a point about normal times, and the balance of economic and ethical reasons for allowing immigration, which Americans will (although it may seem far off right now) once again face in the future. And these reasons overwhelmingly point in the direction of relaxing restrictions on immigration. We can divide these reasons into two kinds: self-interested and humanitarian reasons.

Consider first the familiar humanitarian reasons for relaxing immigration restrictions. The differences in life prospects across the US-Mexican border, for example, are the difference between having the option to live in Arizona, California, New York, or Texas, versus Sonora, Chihuahua, and Sinaloa. By OECD estimates, this represents a difference between a median household income of $45,284 and $13,965.[1] And, of course, life in many countries around the world is much worse than Mexico. According to the United Nations Development Program's data, people born in Sierra Leone, for example, have a per capita income of $684 (in 2015 dollars), with more than 60 percent of the population living on less than $1.25 a day.[2]

By far, the best thing we can do for people in these countries is to let them move elsewhere.

The difference is not just financial. To stay alive in Sierra Leone for more than 54 years is already to beat the odds.[3] Where we are born affects our health, the chances of our children surviving past the age of five, our life satisfaction, and much, much more.

By far, the best thing we can do for people in these countries is to let them move elsewhere. History is littered with (sometimes) well-intentioned attempts to "fix" or improve poor societies elsewhere. That history includes at least as many failures as successes. There are few if any stories of foreign aid significantly boosting living standards abroad. The track record of military interventions is worse yet. The one thing that does make a difference is letting people work and live in better places. They want to come here. And typically, they just want to work. It's up to us to let them.[4]

The familiarity of these humanitarian reasons can sometimes obscure another set of reasons: self-interested ones. The case for relaxing immigration restrictions is not only that it's a good thing to do for others. It's not only because the best thing we can do for people from developing countries is to let them seek out a better life for themselves. Indeed, the case for relaxing immigration restrictions is also a self-interested one. It's by far the best thing we can do for the American economy.

When immigrants come to the United States, Americans win as a result. And when immigrants are prevented from coming to the United States, Americans lose. We lose because we can't hire, cooperate with, and interact with the people whom we would like to hire, cooperate with, and interact with. We lose because there are fewer customers in our stores, potential employees who can do work for us, colleagues to rely on, suppliers to buy from, renters to rent to, and so on. Even those who don't directly interact with migrants lose as a result of restrictions. The balance of empirical evidence indicates that immigration has almost entirely positive economic effects for Americans. The only drawback may be temporary negative effects on wages for a small group of American workers. But these disappear over time and are vastly outweighed by the positive impact for others.[5]

When immigrants come to the United States, Americans win as a result.

From an ethical point of view, the fact that both sets of reasons exist matters. The fact that self-interested and altruistic reasons line up in favor of relaxing immigration restrictions shows that this is a case of mutual advantage. Cases like trade or ordinary cases of exchange are cases of mutual advantage. These are situations in which people typically walk away from a deal feeling better than they did before. Immigration represents a similar situation. It, too, involves people interacting and cooperating in ways that make them better off. The confluence of altruistic and self-interested reasons for relaxing immigration restrictions means this, too, is a win-win proposition. We will benefit from letting people immigrate to our country. And people around the world will benefit as much.

Ethically, when people want to do things that make them all better off, the right thing to do is usually to just let them. In this sense, the question is not whether immigrants have a right to come here. The question is whether we have a right to prevent them. And, absent some compelling circumstance or justification, we simply do not.

To see this, consider the following thought experiment:[6]

> Jane lives in rural Montana. She wants to leave as she is poor and there are not many jobs around. After careful consideration, Jane decides to move to Texas. A willing landlord in Texas is happy to rent her an apartment, and some employers in Texas want to interview her. However, when Jane shows up at the Texan border, she finds Jim blocking the road. Jim, who has long lived in Texas, tells Jane to leave. Jane politely explains that all she wants is to work hard and live in Texas, but Jim is unfazed. When Jane tries to enter Texas anyway, Jim pulls out his gun and forces Jane to turn around.

Clearly, Jim is in the wrong here. Indeed, Jim clearly and grossly violates Jane's rights (in this case, the right to move around freely). He has no business interfering with Jane in this way. As long as she does not threaten or wrong anyone else, Jim should just leave her be. When he forces her to turn around, it is Jim who is in the wrong, not Jane.

Note also that telling Jim to step aside is not equivalent to asking Jim to help Jane. All we're asking of Jim is to refrain from violently interfering with Jane and her freedom (as well as with the people who want to make trades with her). When Jim does use violence and threats of violence to stop Jane, he's actively harming her.

Sometimes, of course, such threats of violence can be justified. We can use violence against criminals. And we can use violence in war. By extension, none of this means that it's never justifiable to use force to restrict immigration. Perhaps there exist good reasons for using force—good enough to deny people their rights to get on with mutually advantageous interactions and exchanges. But such reasons must be established before we can conclude immigration restrictions are acceptable.

The COVID-19 crisis provided just such a justification. The danger of the virus was and is a compelling justification to prevent people from moving. And the reason is that allowing them would greatly increase the risk of a public health crisis. If Jim can tell Jane that he needs to stop her because there's a global pandemic going on, we will think he indeed has a point.

But once that reason is gone, the justification it provides is gone as well. Once the pandemic is over, Jim can no longer rely on it to justify his threats. And in that case, we're back at our question: can Jim stop Jane without seriously and gravely doing her wrong?

One might think that cases like this simply aren't relevant for immigration. Isn't there an important difference between domestic movement and international movement? Don't people who are already in this country have a right to move freely? And don't people outside lack such a right? But note that this argument is a perfectly general one. Perhaps Americans don't owe the same to Mexicans, say, that they owe to other Americans. I doubt it, but perhaps I'm wrong. But even if I am wrong, the same would have been true before the present crisis. And so, this (purported) difference does nothing to support continuing restrictions justified by the threat of a virus in a time without that threat.

The differences in life prospects across the US-Mexican border, for example, represents a difference between a median household income of $45,284 and $13,965.

So, the conclusion remains: the ethics of immigration post-COVID will be similar to before. And, as we've seen, the balance of evidence on that question strongly points toward relaxing immigration restrictions. When people want to move here and make us and themselves better off, our job is just to let them.

Indeed, the economic reasons above make the case for relaxing immigration even stronger post-COVID than it was before. We will need a massive economic recovery—something that will require labor, innovation, and investment. In situations like that, we can't afford to leave money on the table. To put it bluntly, we need all the help we can get.

One of the dangers of a crisis is that measures are initially put in place as temporary yet remain thereafter. It's happened before. But it's important to recognize the ethical and economic truths underlying the question of immigration. It's one thing to restrict people's freedom in the face of a potentially deadly pandemic. It's quite another to restrict their freedom as a matter of course. The former is a good idea. But it does nothing to help justify the latter. When the crisis is over, we need to relax immigration restrictions quickly.

Bas van der Vossen is an associate professor in the Smith Institute for Political Economy and Philosophy, as well as in the Philosophy Department at Chapman University.

Endnotes

1 Organization for Economic Cooperation and Development, "Income," in OECD Better Life Index (database), accessed October 26, 2020, http://www.oecdbetterlifeindex.org/topics/income/. The US Census Bureau offers a significantly higher estimate of US median household income of $53,657. See: Carmen DeNavas-Walt and Bernadette D. Proctor, *Income and Poverty in the United States: 2014* (Washington, DC: US Census Bureau, September 2015), http://www.census.gov/content/dam/Census/library/publications/2015/demo/p60-252.pdf.

2 United Nations Development Program, "About Sierra Leone," UNDP, accessed October 26, 2020, https://www.sl.undp.org/content/sierraleone/en/home/countryinfo.html.

3 World Health Organization, "Sierra Leone," WHO, accessed October 26, 2020, http://www.who.int/countries/sle/en/.

4 For detailed discussions of the empirical evidence for these claims, see Bas van der Vossen and Jason Brennan, *In Defense of Openness: Why Global Freedom Is the Humane Solution to Global Poverty* (Oxford, UK: Oxford University Press, 2018); Fernando Tesón and Bas van der Vossen, *Debating Humanitarian Intervention: Should We Try to Save Strangers?* (Oxford, UK: Oxford University Press, 2017).

5 Rachel M. Friedberg and Jennifer Hunt, "The Impact of Immigrants on Host Wages, Employment, and Growth," *Journal of Economic Perspectives* 9, no. 2 (Spring 1995): 23–44; Simonetta Longhi, Peter Nijkamp, and James Poot, "A Meta-Analytic Assessment of the Effect of Immigration on Wages," *Journal of Economic Surveys* 19, no. 3 (2005): 451–77; Simonetta Longhi, Peter Nijkamp, and James Poot, "The Impact of Immigration on the Employment of Natives in Regional Labour Markets: A Meta-Analysis" (IZA Discussion Paper No. 2044, IZA Institute of Labor Economics, Bonn, Germany, March 2006), https://www.iza.org/publications/dp/2044/the- impact-of-immigration-on-the-employment-of-natives-in-regional-labour-markets-a-meta-analysis; Liesbet Okkerse, "How to Measure Labour Market Effects of Immigration: A Review," *Journal of Economic Surveys* 22, no. 1 (February 2008): 1–30; Simonetta Longhi, Peter Nijkamp, and James Poot, "Joint Impacts of Immigration on Wages and Employment: Review and Meta-Analysis," *Journal of Geographical Systems* 12, no. 4 (December 2010): 355–87; Sari Pekkela Kerr and William R. Kerr, "Economic Impacts of Immigration: A Survey," *Finnish Economic Papers* 24, no. 1 (Spring 2011): 1–32, https://www.hbs.edu/faculty/Pages/item.aspx?num=40774.

6 For the thought experiment, as well as for a more detailed discussion of these issues, see van der Vossen and Brennan, *In Defense of Openness*, chapters 2–4.

CHAPTER 13

Immigrants Truly Make America Great (and without them, that greatness is at risk)

Jack A. Goldstone

On May 30, 2020, President Trump celebrated the launch of America's first manned space mission in almost a decade: "Today we launch American astronauts on American rockets from American soil," he said. Yet he failed to note that the American who made it possible was a naturalized citizen who entered the country as an immigrant.

Elon Musk was born in Pretoria, South Africa. His parents divorced when he was 10 years old. When he was 20, without a degree, he applied to the University of Pennsylvania, where he was admitted and completed undergraduate degrees in economics and physics. In 1995, after dropping out of graduate school at Stanford, he started his first company, Zip2, which he sold to Compaq in 1999 for $341 million. Three years later, Musk became a US citizen. He then went on to found PayPal, Tesla Motors—America's most valuable carmaker—and SpaceX, the first private company to launch Americans into space.

Yet today, a young Elon Musk would not be able to readily gain American citizenship. In response to concerns regarding COVID-19, President Trump has essentially ended immigration to the United States. On April 22, the president signed a two-month ban prohibiting anyone outside the United States, excepting current spouses and children of US citizens, from obtaining permanent resident status. The goal of this proclamation was to prevent such new permanent residents from competing with existing US citizens and permanent residents for jobs during the coronavirus recovery.[1]

Trump's purpose, he claims, is to protect jobs for Americans as we emerge from the coronavirus-induced lockdown. Yet there have also been suggestions that such limits on immigration could be made permanent.[2] If Trump's goals are jobs and economic growth, he needs to rethink his approach to immigration. In American history, figures like Elon Musk are not the exception but are more commonly the rule. Without immigration, America's economy would not enjoy the performance that has made it the world leader in innovation and technological growth.

There are, of course, many proposals to focus America's immigration on higher-skilled workers, or those recruited by tech firms, universities, or other employers because they have established credentials and skills. The president's proclamation itself emphasizes that where there are pressures on the job market, they would come mainly from unskilled, uneducated workers who compete with minorities and unskilled workers in the United States. It seems that the objective of using immigration to strengthen the economy without hurting US workers could then be best satisfied by discouraging and denying permanent residence to immigrants without exceptional skills, and limiting them to temporary work visas.

Reflecting on the history of America's immigration experience reveals the real costs of adopting such an immigration model. Let us look at the stories of five unskilled immigrants who, like Elon Musk, entered America without any degrees or established skills, but found their way to American citizenship. What would have been the consequences had they been turned away and sent home?

In 1848, Andrew Carnegie left his home in Fife, Scotland, with his family at the age of 13, having no formal education. His father—a weaver who was put out of work by weaving machines—came to America and worked in a cotton factory. Young Andrew was determined to escape poverty, worked tirelessly to read and better himself, and became a telegraph operator. Quickly advancing, he helped organize the Union's military telegraph system during the Civil War. Afterward, he worked for the railroads and saw the potential of steel over iron for rails and construction. He began investing in steel mills, and with his partner, H. C. Frick, built the Carnegie Steel Corporation. Carnegie's businesses created one of the largest fortunes in US history. Not only did his steel mills provide jobs for many thousands of workers, his steel fed other industries employing hundreds of thousands more. Carnegie's legacy is apparent on America's main streets today. Universities, museums, libraries, Carnegie Hall, research institutions, and charitable endowments still bear the name of the once lowly Scot.[3]

Without immigration, America's economy would not enjoy the performance that has made it the world leader in innovation and technological growth.

Friedrich Trump was born in Bavaria in 1869. He immigrated to the United States at age 16 with no formal education and started working as a barber. In the 1890s, he moved to the Northwest and made a fortune catering to the needs of new settlers and miners. Friedrich then moved to New York and began investing in real estate in Queens. He bequeathed a growing real estate empire to his sons Frederick C. Trump and John G. Trump. His grandson, Donald J. Trump, became a billionaire real estate developer and the 45th President of the United States.

Mario Rubio Reina (born in Havana, Cuba, in 1925) and his wife, Oriales Garcia Rubio, migrated to the United States in 1956 to look for better opportunities. Mario and his wife initially settled in Miami but then moved to Nevada, where Mario worked as a bartender and Oriales as a housekeeper in hotels and casinos. They eventually returned to Miami, applied for American citizenship, and were naturalized in 1975. Meanwhile, their son Marco, who was born in Miami, went to high school, college, and law school in Florida. He interned for US Congresswoman Iliana Ros-Lehtinen and later ran for office himself. Showing remarkable political abilities, he rose to become speaker of the Florida House of Representatives, and then a US Senator from Florida.

András István Gróf was born in Hungary in 1936. After surviving World War II and the Hungarian uprising of 1956, Gróf fled across the border to Austria. He eventually made his way to the United States where, though almost penniless and speaking hardly any English, he was admitted as a refugee from communist oppression and was able to find work as a busboy in a resort in the Catskill Mountains. Gróf had a passion for education and enrolled at Hunter City College in New York, where he earned a degree in chemical engineering. On graduation, he was admitted to the PhD program in chemical engineering at UC Berkeley. In 1967, after working for a few years at Fairchild Semiconductor, Gróf—who had by then changed his name to Andrew Grove—wrote a college textbook on semiconductors. He was then recruited by Gordon Moore to be one of the first three employees of a new startup called Intel. Under Grove's leadership as CEO, Intel became the world's leading producer of microprocessors and one of the dominant companies in the new world of computing technologies.

Jan Koum was born in Ukraine in 1976 to a poor household, without running water. When he was 16, his mother took him to America to avoid the anti-Semitism in their hometown. They lived in a small apartment in Mountain View, California, where they needed food stamps to get by. Koum's mother worked as a babysitter, and Jan worked in a grocery store after school. But Jan was fascinated by computers and borrowed manuals from a local store and read them eagerly while in high school. After graduating, Koum enrolled at San Jose State University and used his computer skills to get a job as a security tester at the accounting firm Ernst & Young. In 1997, Koum moved to Yahoo!, where he worked for nine years. After being rejected in applying for work at Facebook, he took off work to travel and saw an opportunity in writing apps for Apple's new iPhone. In 2009, Koum started a business to develop his idea of an app: WhatsApp. Five years later, Facebook purchased his company for $19 billion. WhatsApp now provides communications for hundreds of millions of users.

The stories of Carnegie, Trump, Rubio, Grove, and Koum all illustrate the prosperity that immigrants bring. In each case, billions of dollars of wealth, millions of jobs, major technological innovations, and important political leadership would never have existed in our country if the sole criteria of admission to America was having specific technical skills.

Immigrants or their children have been one of the key factors driving America's economic growth for as long as we have been a nation. The facts are remarkable. In a survey of the contributions of immigrants across American history, Michael Neidert noted that "one in four American entrepreneurs are immigrants; 40 percent of new companies have an immigrant involved in their founding; and of the 2017 Fortune 500 list companies, nearly half were founded by immigrants or their children."[4] In a detailed examination of the impact of immigrants on America's economy during the previous surge of immigration in 1850–1920, a period when there was no selection of immigrants based on skills and when almost all immigrants lacked formal credentials, Sandra Sequeira, Nathan Nunn, and Nancy Qian find that "locations with more historical immigration today have higher incomes, less poverty, less unemployment, higher rates of urbanization, and greater educational attainment. The long-term effects appear to arise from the persistence of sizeable short-term benefits, including greater industrialization, increased agricultural productivity, and more innovation."[5]

The problem with skills-based immigration is that it focuses on skills for which there are easily presented credentials, such as a university degree or an already developed talent. It wholly overlooks the drive to succeed that often comes from growing up in poverty, and it can in no way anticipate the accomplishments of young children who grow up to be presidents, senators, or titans of industry. If America had not been willing to take a chance on some immigrants and refugees who did not show obvious talents, the chances are that the country would have missed out on *all* of the accomplishments of the families listed above.

But it will be said that we cannot let just anyone and everyone enter the United States; we will lose our national character; we will never be able to absorb them or employ them. That seems extremely unlikely. The fact is that the number of jobs available in the United States will depend upon the number of thriving businesses created by risk-taking entrepreneurs. These are people who can absorb set- backs and bounce back, can visualize new ways of doing things, and will persevere through challenges—precisely the skills that often mark immigrants and refugees. In fact, the long-term outcome of the COVID epidemic may be the loss of hundreds of thousands of jobs in restaurants, hotels, retail, and other travel and service industries. If we do not have *new* industries, driven by entrepreneurs like Carnegie, Grove, and Koum, we will not have jobs tomorrow for Americans who are here today.

Without immigration, America faces tough headwinds.

Moreover, the US labor force is rapidly shrinking and will have difficulty providing enough workers (and their taxes) to pay down America's rapidly ballooning debts. According to US census projections, if the United States adopted a zero-immigration policy (for permanent residents), the US population will *decline* by almost seven million people from 2020 to 2060. But that is only part of the story.[6] When we look at the detailed projections by age, the working-age population (18–64) is projected to fall by over 24 million people in the next 40 years. At the same time, as baby boomers retire, America's over-65 population will increase by 35 million, putting pressure on our Social Security and Medicare programs, which are supported by payroll taxes on workers. By contrast, under a high immigration scenario, the number of working-age Americans would increase by *slightly more* than the number of Americans over 65, avoiding a massive burden on declining numbers of younger people having to support ever-larger numbers of seniors.

Under the current immigration projection, the United States projects that Social Security and Medicare will run out of resources shortly. According to their trustees, the surpluses set aside to deal with the retiring baby boomers will run out in just a few years: Medicare will become insolvent in 2026; Social Security's retirement and survivors fund will be bankrupt by 2034.[7] Both programs will then have to either cut benefits by one-quarter or more or raise payroll taxes by a quarter or more to maintain current benefit levels. These projections also assume that Americans will continue to have children at a healthy rate of 1.95 children per woman. But in 2019, *actual* fertility fell to a record low of 1.71, or 12 percent less.[8] These projections were all made before the COVID-19 lockdown and its devastating effect on workers' incomes and payroll taxes.

In short, without immigration, America faces the tough headwinds of a fast-shrinking labor force, even as it deals with larger debts from the COVID-19 crisis and rising obligations for Social Security and Medicare to support growing numbers of seniors.

How many immigrants would be needed to achieve a balance whereby the size of the working-age population keeps pace with those over 65? Not as many as one might think. Today, the percent of American residents who are foreign-born is 13.6 percent, and over three-quarters of those are lawful permanent residents and naturalized US citizens.[9] Under the US Census Bureau's "high immigration" projection described above, the fraction of foreign-born residents would increase to 21.6 percent by 2020.

That is higher than today's level. But the world today is one of aging societies that will depend more on immigration. For comparison, several countries that are enormously successful today have a similar or greater percentage of foreign-born residents: Switzerland (30 percent), Canada (21.5 percent), Australia (29 percent).[10] Thus America could adopt policies providing for a relatively high immigration scenario, which would significantly improve the ratio of workers to seniors and better enable America to grow, provide jobs, and pay its debts. Policy could achieve all this and still adopt a legal limit such that the foreign-born would not exceed 25 percent of the total population. That should relieve anxiety that the foreign-born would never overtake the native-born population. Moreover, America has proven extremely capable of assimilating immigrants. Like the penniless, non-English-speaking András István Gróf, who became CEO Andy Grove, immigrants generally adopt American names and become enthusiastic American citizens.[11]

America has been unique in being both the best country in the world to start a business and being relatively open to aspiring entrepreneurs and professionals from around the world. This has made coming to America the goal of the world's most innovative and ambitious individuals and enabled America to stay on the leading edge of technological development for several generations.[12] It is no accident that in the 1980s and 1990s, while other countries were trying to catch up to America's leadership in mass production and consumer goods, American entrepreneurs—including such immigrants or children of immigrants as Steve Jobs (Syrian father, co-founder of Apple), Sergey Brin (Russian-born, co-founder of Google), and Jeff Bezos (raised by a Cuban stepfather, founder of Amazon)—were launching a whole new frontier of the digital economy.

So yes, by all means, let us create additional immigration slots for individuals with visible skills or capital. Let us also set aside slots for foreign students, especially those who graduate from American universities and want to use their skills to start or help build companies in the United States. But at the same time, let us also retain a sufficient number of openings for a mix of individuals striving for success from all countries around the world to bet on the future of America with immigrants. We have always done so throughout our history. We would pay a terrible price if we suddenly stopped banking on this element that truly made America great.

Jack A. Goldstone is the Virginia E. and John T. Hazel, Jr., Chair Professor of Public Policy at George Mason University.

Endnotes

1 Donald J. Trump, Proclamation Suspending Entry of Immigrants Who Present Risk to the US Labor Market during the Economic Recovery following the COVID-19 Outbreak, April 22, 2020, https://www.whitehouse.gov/presidential-actions/proclamation-suspending-entry-immigrants-present-risk-u-s-labor-market-economic-recovery-following-covid-19-outbreak/.

2 Michael D. Shear and Maggie Haberman, "Trump's Temporary Halt to Immigration Is Part of Broader Plan, Stephen Miller Says," *New York Times*, April 24, 2020, https://www.nytimes.com/2020/04/24/us/politics/coronavirus-trump-immigration-stephen-miller.html.

3 Full disclosure: I was named a 2020 Carnegie Foundation Fellow.

4 Michael Neidert, "How 12 Immigrant Entrepreneurs Have Made America Great," *Medium*, August 8, 2018, https://medium.com/@michael.neidert/how-12-immigrant-entrepreneurs-have-made-america-great-ed178fe9837d.

5 Sandra Sequeira, Nathan Nunn, and Nancy Qian, "Immigrants and the Making of America," *Review of Economic Studies* 87, no. 1 (January 2020): 382–419, https://doi.org/10.1093/restud/rdz003.

6 Sandra Johnson, *A Changing Nation: Population Projections under Alternative Immigration Scenarios* (Washington, DC: US Census Bureau, February 2020), https://www.census.gov/library/publications/2020/demo/p25-1146.html.

7 Centers for Medicare and Medicaid Services, *2020 Annual Report of the Boards of Trustees of the Federal Hospital Insurance and Federal Supplementary Medical Insurance Trust Funds*, April 22, 2020, https://www.cms.gov/files/document/2020-medicare-trustees-report.pdf; Social Security Administration, *The 2020 Annual Report of the Board of Trustees of the Federal Old-Age and Survivors Insurance and Federal Disability Insurance Trust Funds*, April 22, 2020, https://www.ssa.gov/OACT/TR/2020/tr2020.pdf.

8 Gaby Galvin, "US Births Continue to Fall, Fertility Rate Hits Record Low," *US News and World Report*, May 20, 2020, https://www.usnews.com/news/healthiest-communities/articles/2020-05-20/us-births-continue-to-fall-fertility-rate-hits-record-low.

9 Jynnah Radford, "Key Findings about US Immigrants," Pew Research Center, June 17, 2019, https://www.pewresearch.org/fact-tank/2019/06/17/key- findings-about-u-s-immigrants/.

10 United Nations, "International Migrant Stock: The 2017 Revision" (dataset), UN Population Division, https://www.un.org/en/development/desa/population/migration/data/estimates2/estimates17.asp.

11 Ran Abramitzky, Leah Platt Boustan, and Katherine Eriksson, "Cultural Assimilation during the Age of Mass Migration" (NBER Working Paper No. 22381, National Bureau of Economic Research, Cambridge, MA, September 2017), https://www.nber.org/papers/w22381.

12 William R. Kerr, *The Gift of Global Talent: How Migration Shapes Business Economy and Society* (Stanford, CA: Stanford University Press, 2018).